Praise for Brett Dufur's *Kat*

"Dufur seems to have picked up a few pointers from William Least Heat Moon, whose *Blue Highways* and *PrairyErth* achieve depth through historical anecdotes and colorful character descriptions . . . For day-trippers as well as long-distance bikers and hikers, the *Katy Trail Guidebook* is a worthwhile investment. They will do well to make room for it in an easily accessible pocket."
— *Christopher Ryan*
Ozark Sierran

"Where most guidebook authors finish, Dufur is just getting warmed up. . . . This book contains fun facts not even a history teacher would know."
— *Chuck MacDonald*
St. Louis Times

"The *Katy Trail Guidebook* is a 'must have' for anyone interested in our Missouri heritage. The book is more than a guidebook for bicyclists and walkers . . . it is also an insightful look at the history of the Katy Railroad and the many small communities that grew up along the railroad."
— *Franklin McMillan*
Antioch Publication

"The guidebook is readable, thorough and permeated with a tone of in-fectious mirth."
— *R. C. Adams*
Boone County Journal

"Dufur's guide gives a feel for the towns with his insightful descriptions and photographs. He uses imagery to portray what is to be found there."
— *Veronica Del Real*
Missourian Weekend

"Dufur, a reporter by schooling, has an eye for stories. . . . And after a long jaunt through Latin America, he knows the value of a good guidebook."
— *Lisa Groshong*
Columbia Daily Tribune

Other Books in the Show Me Missouri Series:

The Complete
*K*ATY TRAIL
GUIDEBOOK

Updated and Revised Third Edition

By Brett Dufur
Illustrations by Kerry Mulvania

In the end we will conserve only what we love;
we will love only what we understand;
we will understand only what we are taught.

— Baba Dioum
Senegalese Conservationist

Project support by Pebble Publishing staff:
Addie Adams, R.C. Adams, Brian Beatte, Tawnee Brown, Brett Dufur,
Daisy Dufur, Mark Flakne, Kari Grawe, Pippa Letsky and Heather Starek

ISBN 0-9646625-0-7 14.95

Cover photograph by Terry Barner. Photographs on back cover by
Steve Wright. B&W portrait by Julie Menendez.

First Edition Printings, May 1995 & July 1995
Second Edition Printing, March 1996
Third Edition Printing, February 1997

Pebble Publishing, P.O. Box 431, Columbia, MO 65205-0431
Phone: (573) 698-3903 Fax: (573) 698-3108
E-Mail: pebble@showmestate.com
Online: katytrail.showmestate.com & Trailsidebooks.com

Printed by Ovid Bell Press, Fulton, Missouri, USA

This book is dedicated to my parents and Ted Jones, father of the Katy Trail. It is also dedicated to the memory of Elizabeth Winters, who continues to inspire me.

Acknowledgments

To everyone who has taken a moment, an hour or in some cases a day to answer one of my questions, I thank you all.

A few names come easily to mind: Derek, who first introduced me to the Missouri River and the Katy Trail, historically, spiritually, culturally and otherwise. Thanks go out to Sally at the Capitol, Harlean, Jody and Ron of Rivercene, Bill Oliver, Jan and Marti of Rocheport for guidance early on and to Mrs. Turner of Tebbetts. Also, to Robert and Maggie Riesenmy, for slowing me down on a few days and refocusing me on the beauty instead of the busy. You were always ready to share your wisdom and a spare fishing pole. Thanks to Ed Yuille, too, whose work in Sedalia paved the way for the Katy Trail . . . he will be missed.

A hearty thanks go out to Dave Lionberger and Lynn Coe from North Oak Print Shop and Bindery for the countless hours they've spent pulling this rookie through the trenches of book publishing. Also, the help from Crystal Cornell, Ted Klaassen, Stacy Downs and John Beahler in editing my poetic verbage was greatly appreciated and sometimes successful. And thanks to the many photographers who shared their vision: Brian Storm, R.C. Adams, Terry Barner, Steve Wright, Keith Simonsen, Nhat Meyer and Julie Pomerantz. Their photo credits are listed in the back of the book.

Dad, thanks for believing in this project from the get-go. Your words and honey-and-peanut-butter toast came in handy at some crucial moments. And to Mom, for repositioning this book for prominent display at every bookstore you've visited. I couldn't have done this without you! Thanks go to my sister to, who stands for all that is right in this world.

Before this book came the trail — and before the trail — the Department of Natural Resources. The entire DNR staff deserves a thanks from all of us who pass serene afternoons on the trail, without a thought to the thousands of hours of hard work that make the Katy Trail a reality. Without DNR, there would be no Katy.

Thanks to Jim Denny, of the Department of Natural Resources, whose countless years of experience and research provided some rich historical insight. Without his help, this book would not have been possible.

Also, special thanks go to David Kelly, Sue Holst and Kristin Allan, of the Department of Natural Resources, for reviewing information about the Katy Trail State Park for this updated and revised third edition.

And to my dog Daisy for reminding me through chewed-up pens and notebooks to get back to the trail when I found myself staring blankly at the computer screen. You were never far behind.

Preface from the author:
Letter from Mile Marker 227

When I was a kid, I used to annoy my parents with questions like "How much does that mountain weigh?" Age has failed to cure me of this terminal curiosity. I wrote this book in part to answer my own burning questions as well as those of others about the people, places and things I saw while walking and biking along the Katy Trail.

What I've learned is that the Katy Trail isn't enjoyed just by cyclists. You might meet "walking clubs" from Oregon or hikers from the Netherlands. Some people prefer to see this beautiful scenic strip by car and drive from town to town and some even do it by canoe.

This book is designed to enhance everyone's experience on the trail. For bikers planning week-long vacations, for hikers on break wanting to learn more about a certain town up ahead and for families who have a kid with a thousand questions, this book is for you. Next time your kid asks — or the kid in you asks — a question on the trail, look inside here, the answer may already be at your fingertips.

Since more and more trail users are coming from beyond Missouri's borders, this updated and revised third edition is packed with extra information needed to plan a trailside vacation from afar. In addition to adding more lodging and camping information, I've updated contact phone numbers in each town and added the post office's phone number when available. Oftentimes, the postmaster knows all the doin's in the smaller towns, or can quickly suggest someone who does.

Since the Katy is still young, the businesses along the trail tend to ebb and flow much like the Missouri River itself. Many new businesses will be springing up and a few may close their doors for good. Before setting hard-to-meet expectations, call a few numbers to check out your route ahead of time, since festival dates and services have been known to change. Area chambers of commerce will have a complete listing of events to help you plan your trip.

Since a fruitful trip along the Katy involves more than perusing mileage charts and phone numbers, the *Katy Trail Guidebook* evolved into much more than just a simple number-filled guide. The Missouri River bottoms are populated with some amazing people, history and trivia. The longer profiles, stories and newspaper excerpts are included for those rainy day armchair odysseys.

This book is a grand introduction to the Katy Trail and life along the Missouri River. A few numbers may be wrong, and as I quickly learned, town history tends to vary as much as the person relating it. A 200-mile trail so steeped in history could easily take a lifetime to research. If I left something out, drop me a line.

Before you hit the trail, don't forget to check out the back of this book . . . there are money-saving coupons, mileage charts and all sorts of other information.

Now, hike and bike with this book. Fold it, draw on it, use it for a pillow when you're camping or for shimming up a table at lunch . . . use it 'til it's dog-eared and then give it away. I hope you enjoy using this book as much as I enjoyed writing it. See you on the trail!

Brett

Katy Trail Guidebook
CONTENTS

Pull-out map of entire trail in back

Katy Trail Guidebook
CONTENTS

TRAILS OF DUST
The History of the Katy Railroad

❖

By Amy Kerby of the *Columbia Missourian*

D esolate on this gray afternoon, the MKT Trail reveals little of what it used to be. Only the wooden trestles and the pools of rain in receding twin strips down the dirt and gravel path hint at the train tracks laid here nearly a century ago.

Something vital is missing. Whispers in this ghostly, hollowed stretch recall an era when locomotives shuddered through rocky outcrops on their eight-and-a-half-mile journey up the Columbia branch of the Missouri-Kansas-Texas Railroad's main line, nicknamed the Katy, along the Missouri River.

The Katy zigzagged out of Fort Riley, Kansas, in the mid-1890s, rushing south into Indian territory and narrowly beating two other railroads in a race where companies laid track almost side by side. Linking Columbia to the eastern division of this Katy line allowed students and businesses access to St. Louis, Kansas City and beyond.

The tracks of the Columbia branch were abandoned in 1985, having carried football teams, business people and WWII soldiers. Eventually, trains lost freight to the truck lines, just as they had lost passengers to the automobile decades earlier. Few reminders remain of those who travelled the Katy Railroad and the men who worked in the sweat of its engines.

Trains were spectacles, intriguing novelties that had seen other parts of the country. It's the feeling of power associated with trains that makes them so fascinating, says Alden Redfield, who is writing a book on the Katy Railroad with his wife, Judy.

"The ground shakes as the train rolls by; you watch the tracks sink as the locomotive goes by. It's darn impressive," he says.

St. Louis papers were tossed from the trains that passed through towns. The trains dropped off hunters at their favorite spots in the woods, took football teams to games and transported students from college back home for the holidays. Train travel was leisurely, a time to acquaint oneself with fellow travellers over lengthy journeys while the land blurred outside the windows.

Tracks spread over the terrain like arteries, infusing life into a growing country. Rather than being centrally organized, the direction of the Katy Trail was often influenced by the willingness of local citizens to finance the construction of branch routes into their home towns.

The few gravel roads in 1890 were nearly impassable for parts of the year, making travel by stagecoach difficult. Steamboats made slow, infrequent trips on the Missouri River. Trains were attractive alternatives: they could quickly cover the same distance regardless of weather.

In the 1880s the Katy was stretching into the Southwest as the rest of the country was being transformed by the Industrial Revolution.

"What they hadn't figured out well was how to get connected back to the East," says Redfield. By 1892, the Katy had found a way. It had a direct route to St. Louis when the company bought two railroad companies that went bankrupt.

Laborers were paid $1.50 a day and fed fresh bread, fruit and vegetables. Most laborers were locally hired black workmen. In 1892, a Holman machine laid the track of the Katy main line, with workmen seeming to move in rhythmic swings a pace ahead of the engine and laying about a mile of track a day in beautifully orchestrated chaos.

History of the Katy Railroad

More common than the track-laying machines were wagons carrying piles of ties, rails and spikes to where workers would lay the track.

"Here's a guy sitting here holding spikes, another guy hitting spikes, another guy wrenching the wrench, you know, and the train is coming," Redfield says. "And you have to be out of the way when the train runs over. If the spikes aren't in, the train's gonna fall off the track. And here come these ties whizzing down, and big heavy rails, and everybody's grabbing them and swinging. It's sorta like a dance, and if everybody's choreographed correctly, they swing through and nobody ever collides. You only collide once in railroading."

Business was steady into the 1940s, when Franklin resident John Holem was a brakeman and engineer on the steam engines. "About 10 a.m. they'd build up the fire, get the engine hot, prepare for the run an hour and a half later," Holem says. They'd go to McBaine for mail, freight and passengers.

Holem grew up in Mokane on the Katy line, immersed in the lingo of the railroad. His father was an extra gang foreman. Holem started on the rails in 1929 doing section work where he fired ditcher machines, which shoveled out trenches to collect mud slides, and spread out the mud. Holem was a fireman, stoking the engine fire, for 25 months before his promotion to engineer.

"It was a good job," Holem says. "Of course, when you get hooked on something, you have things to buy and a family to raise and so forth and so on, well, you stay with it if you can. So I did. I liked railroading."

It was draining, however. "Lot of times you almost froze," Holem remembers. "You're out in all kinds of weather and eat when you could and if you could, even if you wound up eating a mustard sandwich."

Railroaders put in 16-hour days before the "hog law" was passed, which limited them to 12-hour stretches. Engineers never could let their eyes stray from the rails as they watched for objects on the track, oncoming trains or other signs of trouble.

He recalls times when the engines derailed or "got on the ground," and times when people from nearby towns would signal for help after seeing smoke coming from the back of the train that the engineer couldn't see. "They'd get in their pickup truck and haul some water down there to the train," Holem says.

J. B. Garrett of Boonville was a conductor on his first trip to Columbia. He remembers these signs of trouble, too. Hot boxes would occur when axles and journals would lose their lubrication. Garrett found work on the railroad following a period of unemployment. "I was raised on a farm; I didn't care too much for that," he says. "My mom had a cousin over here on the Katy who had friends, and I decided I'd like to ride the rails."

Garrett remembers Southern Methodist University students riding the train from Texas to witness a victory over Missouri in a football game in 1950. On other trips, he talked with lonesome soldiers during WWII, missing home and scared of the journey ahead. He also remembers the St. Louis trains carrying German POWs to Nevada, Missouri.

Hobos also rode the rails, some only keeping two paces ahead of the sheriff from one town to the next, killing chickens or shooting up towns, Judy Redfield says. Garrett clearly remembers one man who broke the pattern. "Occasionally he'd ride up and come to St. Louis. He was always a friendly old fella; we never had to put him off. He had this wooden stub leg — homemade — from the knee down. He could run as good as a two-legged person could to get on the train," Garrett recalls.

Trains were packed tight in those days. But railroads always had viewed passenger service as inconvenient, and in 1957, passenger trains were pulled off the main line to concentrate on hauling freight. Eventually, trucks took over the freight. Although freight trains were a cheaper form of travel, it was more efficient to unload freight directly from a truck to a warehouse's back doors.

"You might say it had to be that way," Holem says. The railroad fascinated

Railside tent towns with names as exotic as Zanzabar followed the progress, and jobs, of the Katy line.

people in its day. "There were fellows who worked on the railroad that felt the same way. I felt that way, too," he says.

When the trains stopped running the branch, "it was just like losing your best hound-dog. I brought the last train off the Columbia branch. That was the last day I worked." Holem retired in 1975. The ties had rotted, and trains were running five miles an hour at the end.

"It had been in operation for 100 years, and [its closing was] kind of a sad thing," Garrett says. "It's where you worked, where you made your bread and butter."

Reprinted from the *Columbia Missourian,* April 4, 1994

History of the
⤸ Katy Trail State Park ⤷

The true spirit of Missouri . . . means a mixture of "muleishness," tolerance, independence and a sense of regard for the rights of every man of goodwill.
— *Walt Disney*

All you need to be assured of success in this life is ignorance and confidence.
— *Mark Twain*

In 1986, the Missouri-Kansas-Texas (MK&T) Railroad (better known as the Katy) ceased operation on its route from Sedalia to Machens. This presented the chance for an extraordinary recreational facility — a 200-mile-long flat hiking and biking trail.

Nationwide, railroads are currently being abandoned at the rate of 2,000 miles per year. Through a Rails-to-Trails program, old railroad corridors are banked for future transportation needs and used on an interim basis as recreational trails.

Though Katy Trail enthusiasts were first met by stiff opposition from many landowners who felt the deeded railroad land should be returned to them, trail proponents eventually won out. Because of a generous donation by Edward "Ted" D. Jones Jr., the Missouri Department of Natural Resources was able to secure the right-of-way. A subsequent donation is allowing further development of the trail.

According to the Rails-to-Trails Conservancy, the number of rails-to-trails conversions across the U.S. has jumped from 75 in 1986 to a current total of 821 in 48 states spanning 8,000 miles of America's most beautiful landscape. There are also another 1,069 in development. Some are short mile-long segments of old railroad line. Others are more lengthy. The Katy Trail, at 185 miles, is America's longest rails-to-trails project.

Rails-to-Trails projects are as diverse as our national landscape. Some, like Seattle's Burke-Gilman Trail, hug urban centers and are used by an estimated 1,000,000 commuters and bikers every year.

By contrast, the Katy Trail is nestled in rural seclusion, allowing hikers and bikers to travel through some of the most scenic areas of Missouri. The majority of the trail follows the Missouri River, beside some of the most fertile agricultural land in the country, and beside towering limestone bluffs. The trail travels through many types of landscapes including dense forests, wetlands, deep valleys, open pastureland and gently rolling farm fields.

Though scheduled for completion in 1994, the flood of 1993 damaged 75 of the original 126 miles. The trail's grand opening (the connecting of east and west trail sections) occurred in September 1996.

There are currently 185 miles of trail open, from Sedalia to St. Charles. Sections from Clinton to Sedalia and from St. Charles to Machens are currently underway and may be completed during the 1997 season.

Missouri Department of Natural Resources Information Hotline:
1 (800) 334-6946 and (573) 751-2479

Missouri River District Office:
(816) 882-8196

For more information on the state of Missouri, contact the Division of Tourism at (573) 751-4133. For trip planning information call 1 (800) 877-1234.

In addition to the phone numbers listed above, phone numbers are listed in each town for additional trailside information. It's a good idea to call ahead and check the weather before you go. It can be perfectly sunny in Sedalia and be raining cats and refrigerators in St. Louis.

Note: In 1996, Mid-Missouri area codes changed from 314 to 573. This book has been updated with the new area codes. Only the St. Louis metro area retains the 314 area code. Clinton, Sedalia and Boonville are still area code 816.

20 Commonly Asked Trail Questions

1. *Who runs this park?*
The Katy Trail State Park is operated by the Department of Natural Resources, which also operates Missouri's 78 other state parks.

2. *Is the trail hilly?*
On the contrary. This site was selected by the railroad for its flatness. Trail grades seldom reach more than 5 percent.

3. *Where's the bathroom?*
Trailheads have bathrooms — from port-a-potties to permanent facilities.

4. *How many miles will I average in an hour?*
Walkers average 1-3 miles an hour. Cyclists 5-20 miles an hour.

5. *May I camp anywhere along the trail?*
No. Camping is only allowed in privately operated campgrounds. See the **Campers' Notes** and **Campground Quick Reference Guide** for information.

6. *Should we take our kids?*
Definitely! Many trailside bike shops even rent bike trailers for toddlers.

7. *Is trailside medical assistance available?*
Medical assistance would come from the nearest town. To assure fast response time, note the nearest mile marker or geographic landmark before going for help.

8. *What is the trail surface like?*
The trail is covered with a fine crushed limestone surface. This rock packs down almost like pavement. Chat can be as hard and smooth as pavement when dry, but be prepared for wash-outs after heavy rains. Beware of soft shoulders.

9. *What happened to the old tracks?*
The Katy railroad sold the salvage rights to an independent company that came in and removed the iron rails and wooden ties.

10. *What's the best time to see wildlife along the trail?*
The best time to spot wildlife is at dawn or at dusk. You may see Red-tailed Hawks soaring above you and American Bald Eagles in the winter. (Missouri has more eagles in the winter than any other state.) Migratory birds, including Great Blue Herons, Sandpipers, Canada Geese and Belted Kingfishers are also common.

If you want to learn about nature along the trail, check out Pebble Publishing's nature guide, also by me. This illustrated beginner's guide identifies commonly seen trees, wildflowers, leaves, birds, wildlife, cloud formations, fossils, footprints, nasty stuff, insects and more. See the back of this book for more information.

11. *Why are the towns so perfectly spaced at 10-15 mile intervals?*
While the railroad was a dependable way to get products to larger markets around the nation, local travel was still primitive and restricted to a few miles. Towns were spaced every ten miles to make the railroad accessible for farmers hauling their products to market.

12. *It's raining again. What's the next best thing to riding the trail?*

Surf up the Missouri and visit the *Interactive Katy Trail* online, where it never rains! For "cyberhikers" around the world! See the back of the book for more info.

13. *I'd like to plan a trip along the trail, but I still have so many questions!*

See the **Bikers Bulletin Board** at the back of the book for more trip-planning suggestions. You can also receive a free color brochure on the Katy Trail from the Department of Natural Resources by calling toll-free 1 (800) 334-6946.

14. *What kind of bike should I bring to ride?*

Most trail riders use mountain bikes for their relatively upright riding position. Many bikers also use ten-speed-style road bikes. Hybrids, which are a cross between mountain bikes and ten-speeds, are also very well suited for the trail. Look throughout the book for additional **Bikers' Notes**.

15. *I'd like to ride the trail but don't own a bike or can't get it to the trail.*

No sweat! There are bike rentals available up and down the trail in many different towns. Mountain bikes, tandems and toddler trailers are among the choices, and prices generally range from $5-10 an hour to $15-20 for the day.

16. *What's the best time of year to come?*

Spring and fall are by far the most popular seasons for extended trips along the Katy. Spring bathes the trail in dazzling greens and the trail is showered with flowering dogwoods and redbuds. Fall is also a favorite season, when sugar maple, sumacs and bittersweets explode in hues of orange and red.

Late March begins the peak time for trail enjoyment and continues on through November. Summers are usually warm and humid. A typical July day, during the hottest month, may be around 60 degrees at sunrise and 85 degrees by midafternoon.

17. *How safe is the trail?*

There are Katy Trail State Park rangers patrolling the Katy Trail. I've never heard of any safety problems along the trail, and given the trail's rural Missouri setting, I don't expect to hear any stories of problems any time soon.

18. *Do I need to bring a bike lock?*

At most trailside stops, your bike should be within sight and fine. I've ridden the trail many times and couldn't even tell you where my lock is at. I've never felt a need for one. At night, I ask the campground or hotel to lock my bike up and that frees me from carrying a bulky lock with me. Obviously, use your own discretion for each situation.

19. *What will I probably forget to bring and regret for the rest of the trip?*

Shades, sunscreen and long-sleeved shirts to screen you from the direct summer sun. Mosquito repellant or Avon's Skin-So-Soft is also helpful.

20. *OK, what will I <u>really</u> regret for the rest of the trip?*

Not having a more padded bike seat. These can be purchased at various trailside bike shops. Or, wrap your extra tire tube around your seat and mildly inflate it for a much more cushy ride. It works!

GETTING STARTED:

• As of March 1997, approximately 185 miles of the trail have been completed from Sedalia to St. Charles. The grand opening of the 185 miles was held at the North Jefferson Trailhead on September 28, 1996.

• Other sections currently under construction include Clinton to Sedalia on the west, which is a 33-mile section of rail corridor donated to the state by the Union Pacific Railroad.

St. Charles to Machens on the east end of the trail is also under construction. These sections may be completed by the end of the 1997 season, allowing the trail to span a distance of 230 miles. Negotiations are also underway that could eventually take the Katy Trail into Kansas City via the Rock Island route.

• The trail is very accessible to physically challenged people. Segments of the trail rarely exceed a 5 percent grade or a 2 percent cross slope. Also, several trailside bike shops rent alternatively styled bikes, making the trail a delightful outdoor adventure for everyone.

• Any questions about development or operations should be directed to the Department of Natural Resources at 1 (800) 334-6946.

CYCLISTS:
Things to bring along:
❑ extra tube
❑ pump
❑ water bottles (2 quarts)
❑ small tool kit (in some areas, bike shops are few and far between)
❑ spare master chain link or extra chain
❑ a padded seat

TRAIL MARKERS:

The old railroad mile markers are long gone, but DNR has since put up new mile markers. Mile marker 227 is located on the west end of the trail in Sedalia and mile marker 27 is located on the east end of the trail at Machens in St. Charles County.

A WORD OF CAUTION:

The Katy Trail is a wonderful place to hike and bike. Much of the enjoyment along the trail comes from exploring and stopping in the many small towns that dot the trail's edge. Just remember as you exit the trail to watch for traffic that may not be watching for you. Obey road signs, respect private property and use reflectors, helmets, bright colors and lights to make your presence known.

ote: The towns in this guidebook are listed from *west to east*, progressing town by town "downriver," covering the trail's entirety to St. Charles and Machens. If you hop on the trail in St. Charles, you'll need to begin at the back of this book and work your way toward the front.

Clinton

Bikes • Camping • Food • Gas • Lodging • Parking • Post Office • Restrooms
Milepost 262
10 miles from Clinton to Calhoun
Clinton Chamber of Commerce: 1 (800) 222-5251
Sedalia Chamber of Commerce: 1 (800) 827-5295
Post Office: (816) 885-5221 • Zip Code: 64735

Whoa! Whoa! Whoa! For now, this trailhead is closed and remains only a loose gravel bed. As of March 1997, Sedalia was still the westernmost completed trailhead for the Katy Trail. I included Clinton, Calhoun, Windsor and Green Ridge in this guidebook for when the trail does finally open up.

The Clinton trailhead is scheduled for completion some time in 1997. Call the Department of Natural Resources for information on trailhead construction here, or continue your drive on to Sedalia to begin your eastern ride.

From the Highway: Take I-70 to Highway 13 South (Exit 49 to Higginsville and Warrensburg). Go south on Highway 13 for close to 45 minutes, passing through Warrensburg. Clinton is approximately 30 minutes past Warrensburg. This country highway has few places for passing and is slow going. In Clinton, turn left on Green. If you hit Highway 18 you've gone too far. Take Highway 52, which then parallels the trail. Look for the railroad bed on the west side of the road. This is the site for the Katy Trail once it is completed, which *may* happen as soon as mid-season 1997.

E a t s

There are more than 25 restaurants in Clinton. If you can't find one you need more than a guidebook.

B i c y c l e   S e r v i c e

Coast to Coast Store
221 East Douglas
(816) 885-4262

Lodging

Best Western Colonial Motel
Highway 7 & 13 Bypass
(816) 885-2206

Bucksaw Point Resort & Marina
670 SE 803 Route 3
(816) 477-3323

Clinton Resort Inn & Convention Center
Highway 7 & Rives Road
(816) 885-6901

Campgrounds

Bucksaw Park
Highway 7 & State Road U
(816) 438-7317

Hickory Hollow Resort
RR 2 — ½ mile north of Highway 7 on Route PP
(816) 477-3413

Clinton was named for DeWitt Clinton. For a few years in the late 1800s, Clinton was home to Baird College for Women, which encouraged thrift. "Extravagance in youth leads to poverty in old age," says its manual.

As you pedal east, you are following the trail much as the original progress was made. The Clinton to Sedalia leg of the Katy Railroad preceded the Boonville leg by three years and the Franklin to Machens leg by nearly 25 years. This section was laid on the partially completed bed of the Tebo and Neosho Railroad, which began back in the 1860s.

As you will soon read, most of the small towns along the Katy Trail were born — and many died — with the railroad. As iron rails were laid through town, they laid a groundwork for the Golden Age of many small Missouri towns.

As James Denny, Missouri's state historian, has written, "There is abundant evidence of this rich flowering of local life in the dozens of towns along the 233 miles of the Katy route thus far examined. Far from devastating small town economies and business diversity, as the automobile age has done, the railroad seemed to bring it to its highest peak of fruition."

This part of the trail was affected by different economic and social forces than the rest of the trail. In contrast to the central and eastern portions of the trail that are heavily steeped in the lore of Daniel Boone, Lewis and Clark, early French trappers and German immigrants, the first 33 miles of the Katy Trail pass through an area settled largely by subsequent waves of pioneers.

Here, well outside of the Missouri River Valley, the trail passes primarily through prairie country, farms and cattle ranches. The route here is relatively secluded, for the most part avoiding roads and houses, and the land is wooded and cut by many small stream valleys. The trail meets up with the Missouri River in Boonville and the two continue on together the rest of the way to St. Charles.

Clinton's restored square is worth a visit. Over 70 percent of the buildings on the square have been revitalized since 1990. The Clinton Area Chamber of Commerce is located in the old Katy Railroad Depot on the southeast corner of the square, and other nearby highlights include an 1800s drugstore and soda fountain, barber shops, doctors offices, old-time bank tellers windows and more.

The Henry County Museum and Cultural Arts Center, at 203 West Franklin Street, is also the center for preserving much of the area's gleaming past. It is open April through December, Tuesday through Saturday, 12 noon - 4 p.m. Call (816) 885-8414 for more information.

Clinton is located about 70 miles from Kansas City and 90 miles from Jefferson City. Clinton has several bluegrass festivals beginning every year in May, at Lester Foster's Music Park, four miles east of Clinton, and an old-time Fourth of July celebration held each year.

A hamlet named Lewis is located between Clinton and Calhoun. Today there isn't much there, despite its name appearing on maps of the Katy Railroad system dating back to 1888. It was probably established as a shipping point for coal extracted from a nearby mine.

Campers' Note: There is camping at Lester Foster's Music Park, (816) 537-7306, $3 a night without electric, $5 per day with electric. It includes hot showers and restrooms and is handicapped accessible. It's four miles east of Clinton on Highway 7. Then go ½ mile south on Highway West.

Scenic Route through Tightwad, Missouri: If you're in tourist mode with wheels, the nearby town of Tightwad is worth a look. Located 15 miles from Clinton, the small town of 50 received its name after the postman left in a huff screaming "Tightwad! Tightwad!" to a local store owner who had sold the postman an exceptional watermelon earlier in the day, only to turn around and sell it again to another customer. The store owner then put another melon in its place, thinking the postman wouldn't notice.

Oddly enough, today there is a huge UMB Bank in Tightwad. I tried to fight the words but they came to my mouth anyway as I talked to a guy that lives there.

"Does it strike you as kinda funny that there's a bank in Tightwad!?!" I asked.

"Actually, people from all over — Chicago, Indiana, Florida — have accounts here so they can get those checks that say 'Tightwad' on 'em," he said.

Off the town square in Calhoun, Deb's Mini-Mart is a good place
to stop for a drink, snacks and some local gossip.

Calhoun

Food • Parking • Post Office • Restrooms
. Milepost 252
10 miles from Clinton to Calhoun • 25 miles from Calhoun to Sedalia
Sedalia Chamber of Commerce: 1 (800) 827-5295
Post Office: (816) 694-3524 • Zip Code: 65323
Directions: I-70 to Route 13 (Warrensburg) to Route 2 to Route J.

Eats

Deb's Calhoun Mini-Mart
105 South Olive
(816) 694-3445

Calhoun, population 450, is known locally as Jug Town. The area once had three pottery companies supporting the local economy because of the high-grade clay located nearby. When fine porcelain dinnerware started to be mass-produced inexpensively in other corners of the world, the industry and town faded into its present state.

"The clay around here is some of the best in the world," said Deb Adams, who runs the Calhoun Mini-Mart. "Here, pottery is THE big deal."

Calhoun is also home to the oldest continuing colt show in Missouri, now in its 87th year. Their Colt Show and Pottery Festival is held each September.

Today's Main Street scene is quiet and subdued. There are some horseshoe pits and a town square, but the town seems to hold tightly to the past.

"The town has actually turned away improvements to the town and roads that wouldn't have cost us a dime," Deb said.

Founded in the 1830s, Calhoun was incorporated in 1870, the year the railroad came through. Its founders had high ambitions and provided for the spacious courthouse square, which still defines the heart of the town. Calhoun, however, was not destined to become a county seat. Clinton, laid out ten miles farther south on the Harmony Mission Road, edged Calhoun out because of its more central location and prosperity.

In 1838, Clinton built a brick courthouse at a cost of $2,000. In 1880 the population was 492. There were 5 general stores, 5 groceries, 2 drugstores, 3 hardware stores, 2 grain dealers, a steam flouring mill, a music store, a dressmaker, a photographer, a sawmill, a hotel, 2 bricklayers, a wagon maker, a broom factory, 5 physicians, a veterinarian, an attorney and a saloon.

Calhoun participated directly in the Industrial Revolution during the railroad age. Thanks to nearby clay deposits ideal for earthenware, by 1880, there were six potteries in full blast making jugs of all sizes, crocks, milk pans and other such ceramics. All of these goods were then shipped to the outside world via the Katy.

If you're coming off the trail, Deb's Calhoun Mini-Mart is the stop for snacks, bait and local gossip.

"People meet in here at the back table to hear who got arrested, who died last night, who was with someone else's wife . . . this is where everyone comes to find out what they need to know," said Deb's mother, Betty.

"I'm the town question mark," Betty said. "I know the why, who did what, to when and to whom."

American Toad
& Bloodroot

Windsor

Food • Gas • Lodging • Parking • Post Office • Restrooms
Sedalia Chamber of Commerce: 1 (800) 827-5295
Windsor Chamber of Commerce: (816) 647-2318
Post Office: (816) 647-2313 • Zip Code: 65360

From the Highway: I-70 to 13 South (Warrensburg exit) through Warrensburg.
Then east on 2 to Windsor.

Eats

Harold's Supermarket

Casey's
500 West Benton Street
(816) 647-9965

The first Confederate flag raised in Missouri was in Windsor. This area was settled by trappers in the early 1800s and was organized into a county before Missouri even became a state. The first railroad to come through, in 1869, was the Tebo & Neosho, later to be known as the MK&T (Katy). During these years, the town prospered along with the railroad.

When Union Pacific bought the Katy Line in 1988, cabooses in use were being discontinued and given to Missouri communities. The caboose located here, built in 1968, was numbered 76. When the Katy Railroad decided to form a bicentennial commemorative train, caboose number 76 was chosen, as was engine number 200. These were the only ones so designated.

Windsor also has had an Amish community for more than 20 years with over 40 families now residing in the area. The Amish live on farms, in modest homes, and travel by means of horse-drawn vehicles. Some run family businesses such as the Kuntry Bulk Store, which is open daily except Thursdays, Sundays and holidays. It carries a large selection of bulk foods, spices and fresh produce. Because of their religious beliefs they do ask that pictures not be taken of them.

The virtues of the town were established early on. From the book *Windsor: A brief description of a good Missouri Town, 1889:*

It is right, prosperous and growing town of 2,000 souls, as neat and fair as a new England village. Full 70 per cent of the people are from the eastern states, Vermont and Ohio being largely represented. Windsor is a town that will do to tie to, especially for the lovers of sobriety, educational advantages and advancing property values.

Windsor was platted in 1855 and had a population of around 300 by the beginning of the Civil War. First called Bellmont, then Spring Grove, Windsor finally found a name it could keep, named after the castle in England. The town emerged from the war badly damaged. It didn't start to take off until the Katy Railroad was built. By the late 1800s, the town had 550 people and some 33 businesses. There were also 2 lawyers, 3 physicians, 7 preachers, 2 churches and no saloon. Ten years later, there were 63 businesses and 6 manufacturing establishments. Windsor had also acquired a newspaper and a grade school. It now boasted 872 inhabitants.

Thirteen hundred railcars loaded with cattle, hogs, hay, oats and other products departed from Windsor in 1888. In 1889, the ratio of churches to saloons had increased to 7 to 0.

The railroad station in Windsor was the Katy's top-of-the-line style in frame construction and indicated the town handled more traffic than the standard design allowed for. It is identical to the depot found in St. Charles.

Campers' Note: Eleven miles from Windsor on Route Y is the Tebo Branch of Truman Lake. There is lakeside camping here, restrooms and a water spigot.

Tufted Titmouse

The "Pride of Windsor" is former MK&T caboose No. 130,
now restored to its original appearance as the Katy Railroad's Spirit of 76.

Discarded Caboose Restored to Its Patriotic Splendor

It's a story newspapers just love to run. Some guy, down on his luck, goes to an auction. He buys a picture — one that looks as if it's been painted by numbers.

An art expert happens to see the painting and recommends restoration. Somebody with thinners and chemicals comes in. The painting is cleaned.

And what emerges? You got it. A Rembrandt. A Homer. A Goya. Naturally, the offers pour in. Big money. End of story.

Of course, that doesn't happened that often. Except . . .

Not long ago a few residents of Windsor thought maybe the old Katy line should be remembered. After all, the Katy had run through here for years.

Eventually the city wrote a letter. Would the Katy contribute a caboose?

And eventually a Katy caboose, painted green and yellow and streaked with rust, arrived. It was placed on a section of track on the east side of town not far from where the old Katy depot once stood. The place is called Katy Park, a place where children will play in future years.

The number on the side of the caboose was 130. It was just an old caboose, one that looked like a thousand others in parks throughout the land. Nobody would have said a thing if the folks here had just sort of touched it up and left it the way it arrived. Except . . .

"We decided it needed cleaning," says Q.W. Schroer, 69, who worked for the Katy 42 years and retired here. "So we got in a sandblaster."

The sandblaster began sandblasting. And underneath the green and yellow paint, believe it or not, stripes and stars started to appear. As if by magic.

"Well, people started looking at me as if I had St. Vitus' dance," Schroer says.

"I was just going crazy, doing everything but back flips. At my age, too."

What was underneath the paint was the Katy's contribution to the bicentennial year of 1976 – a caboose painted white with a huge American flag on each side. Letters brought out by sandblasting gave the name of the car, "Spirit of '76."

The sandblasting also revealed that the original number of the caboose, built by the Darby Corp. in Kansas City, Kansas, wasn't No. 130. It was No. 76. Made sense. Caboose No. 76 became the "Spirit of '76."

Once Schroer got himself calmed down, he figured, as chairman of the caboose project, that the thing to do was repaint the old car in its bicentennial colors.

Which has happened. The caboose now fairly blinds passing motorists, all red, white and blue.

Why? Well, for a lot of people, the bicentennial lasted just so long. But others still remember sort of a wondrous time when even a company as massive as a railroad could get into the act and with a few gallons of paint say for all to see that being an American wasn't all that bad of a deal.

So Windsor not only got a caboose. It got something that was absolutely special. Schroer, of course, knew all about the caboose. At home he had a picture, taken in Oklahoma City back then, of him and one of his granddaughters, posing by the very same caboose that now sits in Katy Park.

"Wasn't any problem to restore it once people knew what was underneath that grime," Schroer says. "I walked around town and came up with $3,000. Just like that."

The caboose will be a tourist information center and a small museum. And a tourist attraction. People already are stopping and taking pictures of it.

Schroer says the local garden clubs will decorate the park. And the community betterment club will redo the inside. "It's going to be real nice," Schroer says. "Something people can be real proud of."

Reprinted from "Town Restores Discarded Caboose to Its
Patriotic Splendor," *The Katy Flyer* 13 *(*March 1991*)*

Windsor Review paper debuts on Leno's Tonight Show

The city of Windsor and the *Windsor Review* were on national television in September 1996.

Jay Leno, host of the Tonight Show on NBC, mentioned the town and news paper and held a copy of the newspaper up in front of the cameras.

Leno showed the *Review* during a segment he regularly does on bloopers or funny items found in local newspapers around the United States.

Showing a copy of the September 5, 1996, issue of the *Review,* Leno read part of a front page story that detailed how two men had attempted to pass a fraudulent prescription at Merryfield Pharmacy in Windsor.

"The attempt was foiled when neat handwriting on a prescription appeared suspicious to pharmacist Bill Merryfield," read Leno with a laugh.

Excerpt from the *Windsor Review,* September 27, 1996

Green Ridge

Bike Repair • Food • Gas • Lodging • Parking • Post Office • Restrooms
Sedalia Chamber of Commerce: 1 (800) 827-5295
Post Office: (816) 527-3385 • Zip Code: 65332
From the Highway: I-50 then go south on 127
(between Knob Noster and Sedalia) to Green Ridge.

Eats

Chatter Box Café
104 West Main • (816) 527-3681
Mon.-Thur. 7 a.m. - 5 p.m., Fri.-Sat. 7 a.m. - 7 p.m., Sun. breakfast only

Casey's General Store
Route #1, Box 32 • (816) 527-9309

Ridge Runner Bar and Grill
Cooper Street • (816) 527-3536

Bicycle Service

B & D Tire Service

Whereas Calhoun existed for more than three decades before a railroad came along and Windsor for fifteen years, Green Ridge was purely the offspring of the Katy Railroad. The town is laid out true to the compass on a north-south axis, while the railroad cuts diagonally through the middle of the original town.

Originally called Parkersburg after the Sedalia land speculator Albert G. Parker, this town became Green Ridge in recognition of the site's location on a broad ridge dividing the Lamine and Osage river watersheds.

In order to encourage rapid settlement of the market territory the Katy would create, the Missouri Land Company sent an agent east to tout the virtues of the region. Among the new settlers were a number of Union veterans. Some were hired to help construct the Katy Railroad, and most were staunchly republican.

Like Windsor, Green Ridge considered being "dry" part of being progressive. The town initially had two saloons, but a strong chapter of abolitionists managed to drive the saloon keepers off.

Green Ridge could now proclaim itself a "temperance town in the fullest sense of the word." Almost. If a person really needed a drink it was always possible to get a doctor to prescribe a gallon for "medicinal purposes." The local drugstores would dispense the product properly wrapped with direction for correct dosage.

Almost as distinctive a symbol of the railroad as the depot was the grain elevator. Between 1840 and 1870, grain storage changed from horizontal to vertical — from being bagged and stored in warehouses to being stored in bulk in tall, thin-walled bins. Because grain naturally arches, exerting great forces neither directly downward nor directly to the sides, grain could be stored in relatively weak-walled structures and emptied from the bottom, taking full advantage of gravity.

Such elevators followed the railroad into the Midwest and were the tallest, most visible landmarks of the railroad landscape. Even today, they add gain prominence above many small Missouri towns. Elevators evolved from simple wood framing to concrete and tile construction. Examples of every elevator type are present along the Katy corridor.

Today, Green Ridge's business district is almost entirely extinct. The vacant buildings are mute testimony to the town's once vigorous commercial life.

Between Green Ridge and Windsor, the place name of Bryson still appears on maps. No community or old buildings exist there at present, but at one time the Katy had a branch at this point variously indicated on different maps as Kansas City Junction, Rodelia, or Bryson. In 1895, the Katy built a branch from this point to Holden where its main line out of Kansas City made a junction with the Missouri Pacific. The new branch gave the Katy a direct line into Kansas City and uninterrupted service between that city and St. Louis. The business district of Chilhowee, a town established along that route, has been placed on the National Register in recent years. Nothing remains of that line except for a few traces of the right-of-way that are still shown on USGS maps.

Around Green Ridge, settlement came slowly. Not until the late 1850s did settlers use the prairie for anything more than grazing cattle or cutting prairie hay. The following story tells of the clashes between locals when barbed wire first came into use in the area:

> The fence got patched again, and was regularly cut again. One day, Harry Knapp, then a lad, cut the fence and drove his father's cows in, following them on his pony. The fence builder rode by, saw what he was up to and ordered him out. He threatened the boy with his riding whip. Young Harry, who had prepared for trouble, pulled out an old smith and Wesson 'pepper box' and fired a shot at him. The fence builder fled. It was later found that Harry had creased the top of his head. "I only meant to shoot his hat off" said Harry, when chided by his father . . . This cooled the range war, and brought all to their senses, because nobody wanted to shed blood. However, the upshot was that the fence builder, in later years, passed the scar off as a saber cut which he got in the Civil War, and was granted a pension increase because of the wound he had sustained!
>
> *—A History of the City of Green Ridge, Missouri*

Campers' Note: The city park with shelter could offer primitive camping. There are public restrooms there as well.

Sedalia retains many striking examples of colonial architecture.

Sedalia

Bikes • Food • Gas • Lodging • Parking • Post Office • Restrooms
Milepost 227 • Milepost 224 at Griessen Road Trailhead
25 miles from Calhoun to Sedalia • 9.1 miles from Sedalia to Clifton City
Sedalia Convention and Visitors Bureau: (816) 826-2222
Sedalia Downtown Development: 1 (800) SEDALIA
Chamber of Commerce: 1 (800) 827-5295
Post Office: (816) 826-8887 • Zip Codes: 65301, 65302

From the Highway: From I-70, go south on Highway 65 to Sedalia. To get to the trailhead from downtown Sedalia, go east on Broadway (Highway 50), 11 blocks to Engineer. Turn north (left) onto Engineer and continue 'til you think you're lost, then you'll come to Griessen Road. Turn east (right) and go 2.5 miles.

E a t s

For most of the smaller towns along the trail, every restaurant is listed in this section. Sedalia's large size makes this an impossibility. Though there are no restaurants at the trailhead, Sedalia proper has restaurants to quell every hunger pang.

B i c y c l e   R e n t a l

Bike Werks
on trail across from the train depot
543 East Fifth • (816) 827-0500

Cecil's Cyclery
downtown
704 South Ohio • (816) 826-3987

L o d g i n g

Since it is home to the State Fair, Sedalia has everything available from Hiltons to holes-in-the-wall. These are primarily located downtown.

Riders Brad Straub, Earl Burton and Rodney Naylor, all from Marshall, prefer this end of the trail to the Rocheport leg. "It's not crowded here and there's a few good grades on the trail," Straub said. The end of the trail and the old railroad tracks are visible in the background, where the trail will extend on to Clinton sometime in the future.

Welcome to Sedalia

The westernmost put-in point of the Katy Trail is located three miles outside the city limits, northwest of Sedalia. The compacted fine rock trail surface makes for smooth going. If you've got a little extra time before you begin your ride, it's worth a quick drive through town to see the fairgrounds and check out some of Sedalia's well-preserved architecture. Unlike many towns along the Katy Trail, Sedalia is located far from the Missouri River and therefore still retains many of its earliest structures.

Much of its architecture is listed in the National Register of Historic Places. The historic business center and tree-lined Broadway take you back in time, with many beautifully restored old homes in many different architectural styles, including Gothic, Italianate, Victorian and Queen Anne, dating back to the 1870s and 1880s.

Today, Sedalia is synonymous with the Missouri State Fair. Every August, it plays host to thousands of people upon its fairgrounds. A brochure from the tourism department states that Sedalia is within 500 miles of 20 states. (Try working that into a conversation.)

Founded in 1860, Sedalia became famous as a railroad town and gateway to the West. If you've seen the movie *Rawhide*, you'll recall Clint Eastwood was driving his cattle toward Sedalia. Sedalia is famous as the end of the Texas longhorn cattle drives, which are celebrated every year during Rawhide Days. The Scott Joplin Ragtime Festival each June is another popular event (816) 826-2271.

If you've ever wanted to visit a Missouri "castle" you'll want to check out the Bothwell Lodge State Historic Site, built in 1897, seven miles north of town on 65 Highway. The number there is (816) 827-0510.

The Victorian-style depot station in Sedalia is also worth a visit. It's listed on the National Register of Historic Places. It was built in 1895 and serves as a focal point for the Friends of the Katy's annual Katy Trail Rally at the trail's western terminus. The depot is located at Third and Thompson Streets on the east side of Sedalia, three blocks north of U.S. Highway 50. If you are heading to the Griessen Road trailhead, from Engineer, take East Third Street left one-eighth of a mile to see the old depot. Plans call for restoring the depot and using it as a museum and meeting place and for vendors.

As mentioned earlier, the Katy Trail isn't near the Missouri River here. Sedalia is located in the Broad Bottoms geographic region of Missouri. The trail accompanies the river from Boonville on, which is 35.7 miles northeast of Sedalia. Upon arrival in Boonville, you will be entering what is commonly referred to as the Boonslick region, which will be explained shortly.

Truth, Justice ...
and the American Way

If an untruth is a day old, it's called a lie. If it is a century old, it's called a legend. Such is the case for the following story. Accept it as fable, with a mild cajun mix of fact and fiction . . . And don't try this at home.

I was told this story by an old journalist and river rat. There was once a woman, let us call her Anna Lee, who lived in one of the hollers along the Katy Railroad line between Sedalia and Boonville. She operated a farm there in the early 1900s, and her cattle roamed free across the land, which abutted the Katy Railroad.

Well, it so happened one day she found her prized heifer, Mae-Bell, with four hooves pointing to the Great Almighty, flat on her back, cowbell ringing no more. The only witness had been the sunny sky above, though two steel rails glinted mischievously in the afternoon light.

Anna Lee wrote a terse letter to the president of the railroad, claiming she had a beef to settle. She asked for fair market value for her fallen heifer. She checked her mailbox daily but it seemed to collect only mud daubers, and no letter from the railroad powers-that-be ever found its way to Anna Lee's restless hands.

It just so happens that she lived near the steepest, ugliest, cruelest grade on the entire Katy line — a grade notorious for slowing heavily laden trains. Oftentimes, they brought additional engines in from Boonville to help get the trains up over the steep rise.

Months slipped by with no word from the railroad. Anna Lee pondered justice and its many forms, day and night. One day, she was boilin' fat into lard, stirring up her big black kettle. As she stared into the bubbling brew, a big grease ball popped into epiphany. And she saw the answer to truth, justice and the American way.

The sun was high that day — the day she became a legend. Black churning smoke signaled the first train comin' around the bend. Straining heavily under its load of coal, it slowed as it started up the hill. Little by little it inched up the grade and Anna Lee's lip curled in shrewd satisfaction.

Ten tons of steel and all the technology man could muster failed to match her vengeful brew of liquid fat and fate upon those shiny tracks of progress. The wheels of Engine 1 hit the patch and spun, forward motion denied by gravity's greedy pull. Then, Engine 2 slipped and ceased its forward gait. With wheels spinning uselessly, the entire train began its slow regress.

As the golden dusk faded the horizon, silhouettes of cussing crewmen worked hard into the night to overcome the slippery dilemma. Additional engines were called in from Boonville and Sedalia to push and pull the train over the steep rise. The balance of power and equity is seldom measured by money, and as the railroad quickly learned that day, Anna Lee's cunning was one payback the Katy Railroad could not easily afford.

Clifton City

The uptown and downtown of Clifton City.

Clifton City

Food • Gas • Parking • Restrooms
Milepost 215
9.1 miles from Sedalia to Clifton City • 12.1 miles from Clifton City to Pilot Grove
Trail Information: (816) 366-4240 and (816) 366-4654

From the Highway: From I-70, at the Boonville exit 98,
go south on Hwy 135 to Clifton City.

Eats

Blackie's Daughter's Place • (Refrigerator) Visible from trail.

Clifton City MFA
2 blocks north of trail • Highway 135 & Route BB
(816) 366-4240 • Mon.-Fri. 6 a.m. - 6 p.m., Sat. 6 a.m. - noon, Sun. closed

Clifton City's MFA is a good place to find a cold drink and a cushy bar stool for a brief respite from the afternoon sun. The MFA used to be called Blackie's Daughter's Place. Harlean's dad, Blackie, is well known in the area, so the name of her place just kinda stuck.

Harlean has since moved out of the MFA building and is slowly renovating the old bank closer to the trail. In the meantime, there is a — you're not going to believe this — a refrigerator on the sidewalk chock full of cold pop and candy bars. It's on the honor system and there's a coffee cup in there to hold your change.

The signs hanging from the storefront next door to Harlean's refrigerator will certainly keep you entertained while you revive yourself with a caffeine fix. Storefront signs include: tattoo, real estate, notary public and flea market.

If you really want to prolong your break, do it in the name of history and probe into the intricacies of this town's past. It seems Clifton City lost its post office about 10 years ago and is now, depending on who you ask, actually Otterville. Some say it's just *near* Otterville, and not part of it. Regardless, the story is a good one to tell so we'll just run with it.

The area was known for its otters (obviously) and when the otter population fell near nil, the town was otterly shocked. Everyone chipped in and shipped in a few new ones to repopulate the area.

A mile northeast of Clifton City lies Church Lane, a gravel road crossing. You'll find a white church, a cemetery and a unique, hexagonal, red mule barn off to the left of the trail. Supposedly representing the ultimate in strength, efficiency and modern design, most round barns were built in the Midwest from 1900 to 1910. This part of the trail is particularly peaceful. There is usually little traffic along Highway 135, which parallels the trail at a distance of a quarter mile on and off as they both work their way on to Pilot Grove.

Edna Haynes talks with customer Gina Wells at the Clifton City MFA.

Beverly Hix and Marlys Waller swing away toward dusk
as husbands, Jerry and Bob, talk on.

Pilot Grove

Food • Gas • Lodging • Parking • Post Office • Restrooms
Milepost 203
12.1 miles from Clifton City to Pilot Grove
6 miles from Pilot Grove to Prairie Lick
Gerke's Grocery (across from trail) for trail information: (816) 834-3615
Post Office: (816) 834-6011 • Zip Code: 65276

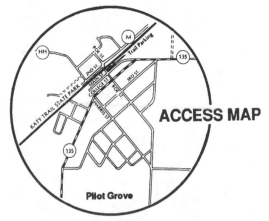

From the Highway: From I-70, at the Boonville exit 98,
go south on Hwy 135 to Pilot Grove.

E a t s

Burwood
Route 1, Box 83

Casey's
Harris & College

Country Junction
RR 1

Dean's Place
137 Main Street

Gerke's Grocery
147 Main Street

Kozy Kitchen
205 Main Street

B e d & B r e a k f a s t
JD's B&B • Roe Street • (816) 834-4630

Pilot Grove, population 714, was one of the early towns to be founded along the Sedalia to Boonville stretch. The Katy Railroad reached Pilot Grove on May 18, 1873, and the town was laid out immediately. Within a decade there were four general stores, one drug store, a hardware store, two tin shops, a furniture store, a saddle and harness shop, three blacksmith and wagon shops, a restaurant, a lumberyard, two hotels, a barber and, of course, a shoemaker.

A total of 317 rail cars of wheat were shipped out of Pilot Grove in 1882. Although the town reaped the benefits of the railroad, these early townships were expected to feed the hand that fed them by turning around and investing in railroad bonds in order to finance the furthering of the rail. Up until 1900, Pilot Grove's taxpayers were paying in principal and interest for a single bond an amount that equalled more than half the township's total assessed wealth. Today the fine rock trail does little to propel the traveller forward. Instead, the parks and places to eat right along the trail make this a perfect place to pass the afternoon.

Bikers' Note: There is also a trailhead at Milepost 197, approximately six miles east of Pilot Grove, called **Prairie Lick**. A parking lot signals your arrival, with another five miles to go to get to Boonville.

. . . The first one to the big shade tree gets to rest the longest . . .

The Katy Trail and the Missouri River come together in Boonville. The Boonville railroad bridge, constructed in 1931, has a 408-foot lift span that was, at the time it was built, the longest in the United States.

Boonville

Food • Gas • Lodging • Parking • Post Office • Restrooms • Trailhead Phone
Milepost 192
5 miles from Prairie Lick to Boonville • 3.6 miles from Boonville to New Franklin
Boonville Chamber of Commerce: (816) 882-2721
Post Office: (816) 882-5666 • Zip Code: 65233

From the Highway: Exit 121 off of I-70.

Eats

Big John's
200 West Ashley Road

Bobber's Restaurant
I-70 & Highway B

Breadeaux Pisa
413 Ashley Road

Casey's
205 Ashley Road

Dad's Restaurant
I-70 & Highway 135

Katy's Fine Dining
Downtown Boonville

Oak Room Café
1004 Main Street

Palace Restaurant
225 Main Street

Riverboat Willy's
203 Main Street

Rome Pizzaria
406 Main Street

Steak House
402 Main Street

Stein House
421 Main Street

Boonville's many bluegrass festivals draw players from
around the country, who play everything from harmonica, guitar
and Missouri's state instrument (the fiddle) to paper bags.

Boonville

Bed & Breakfasts

Doll House
19982 Highway 98
(816) 882-5482
Rates: $45

Morgan Street Repose
611 Morgan Street
(816) 882-7195 or 1 (800) 248-5061
Rates: $65-85

Lady Goldenrod Inn
629 East Spring Street
(816) 882-5764
Rates: $52 couple/ $42 single

River City Inn
311 Spring Street • (816) 882-5465

Rivercene B&B
north of Missouri River Bridge
127 County Road 463
1 (800) 531-0862 or (816) 848-2497
Rates: $80-130

Little Four Oaks Farm
22045 Boonville Road
(816) 882-8048
Rates: $65

Lodging

Apple Tree Inn • Ashley Road
(816) 882-6545

Comfort Inn
I-70 & Highway 5 (Exit 101)
(816) 882-5317

Atlasta Motel • I-70 & Highway 87 (Exit 106)
(816) 882-5686

Ravenswood
Highway 5 • (816) 882-7143

Boonville Inn
I-70 & Highway B (Exit 103)
(816) 882-3467

Super 8 Motel
I-70 & Highway B (Exit 103)
(816) 882-2900

The Missouri River Bridge crossing at Boonville is a breeze, thanks to a separate walkway that's shaky but stable. The new bridge will also have a separate walkway.

Boonville History

Boonville's population of 7,000 allows it to cater to most needs without having to resort to the hustle and bustle associated with most larger cities. Hanna Cole, a widow with nine children, came to this site in 1810 and founded Boonville. She also built the Hanna Cole Fort during the War of 1812.

Boonville is one of Missouri's oldest surviving communities. On June 17, 1861, the first Civil War battle west of the Mississippi River took place here. Walter Williams, the founder of the University of Missouri–Columbia Journalism School, the first of its kind, is buried here, as are many other famous Americans.

In Boonville, there are 450 sites on the National Register of Historic Places, six bed and breakfasts, twenty restaurants, six motels, campgrounds and over 100 antique dealers. In 1869, Boonville gained access to the main line of the Missouri-Pacific Railroad at Tipton. In 1873, the MK&T line reached Boonville and the finest railroad bridge at that point was built over the Missouri River. Boonville's success as a railroad town was further enhanced when the river route of the Missouri-Pacific Railroad was completed in 1901. The early years of this century brought new success to town. During Boonville's heyday of railroad traffic, up to 60 trains per day passed through town.

Boonville is also the town where the folk music tradition lives on. Boonville plays host to folk music festivals throughout the year, which draw locally and nationally known favorites. These festivals are sponsored by the Friends of Historic Boonville, (816) 882-7977, and are performed at Thespian Hall, a pre–Civil War era theater. If at all possible, you should plan your visit to Boonville to correspond with one of these folk festivals. They are wonderful. The Big Muddy Folk Festival takes place every year in April and the Missouri River Festival of the Arts takes place in August.

The last public hanging in Missouri took place in Boonville in 1939. The Old Cooper County Jail, built in 1848, is worth seeing, as is the hanging barn. The Boonville train depot was built in 1912 and is the only surviving example of the railroad's Spanish-style depots. It once even had a red-tiled roof. The Department of Natural Resources and the Boonville Chamber of Commerce are working to restore the structure. The Chamber of Commerce may even relocate its offices to this historic structure.

The Hain family legacy is another interesting side note of Boonville history. The family settled here in 1836. Their house was continually inhabited and expanded by generation upon generation, until 1990, when the last Hain family member died.

Bikers' Note: At Boonville, the Katy Trail deviates from the original railway bed. Since the trail crosses the Missouri River at this point, after reaching the Mission Style depot, built in 1917-1919, follow the Katy signs to the old Missouri River Bridge. There is a walkway on the bridge that will take you across to reconnect with the trail on the north side of the river.

New Boonville Bridge Underway

By Nicole David and Kara Choquette

❖

It's called "functionally obsolete" by Missouri Highway and Transportation Department. But if you've driven on it, you've probably called it "scary." The open-grated Missouri River Bridge in Boonville on Missouri Highway 5 was built in 1923. The narrow two-lane bridge will be replaced in 1997.

"My dad got to see the old one being built, and I get to see this one being built," said Judy Shields, of the Historic Friends of Boonville.

Roughly 70 feet shorter than the old bridge, the new bridge will have two 20-foot-wide vehicle lanes and an 8-foot walkway connecting with the Katy Trail.

Construction began in 1994 and the Jensen Construction Company of Iowa is expected to complete the $17.3 million bridge around August 1997.

"It's taken a while to mobilize because of the type of work this is," said Brian Williams, engineer for the Missouri Highway and Transportation Department. "The barges, the heavy equipment, all those things take a while to move in by river."

Besides the added challenge of having a construction site in the middle of a river, two of the four piers — the ones flanking the navigational channel — will each require eight separate drilled shafts reaching to the rock below the Missouri, he said. Each shaft is 6 feet in diameter.

"A large bridge like this over water, and over the Missouri no less, takes quite a bit more work," Williams said. Unlike its predecessor, the new bridge will be supported from underneath. "I've been in the construction business for 28 years, and this is by far the biggest job I've been around," he said. "You don't see a new bridge go up over the Missouri every day."

Compiled from the *Columbia Missourian,* July 7 and September 7, 1994

A downtown mural painted by Peggy Guest shows the many pioneering groups that passed through this area on their way west. From Boonville through Rocheport, you will be travelling through the region of Missouri called Boonslick country.

Boonslick Country

The "Boonslick" country of central Missouri was the site of the first permanent American settlement west of St. Louis in the 1800s. The name comes from the salt springs known as "Boone's Lick" where Daniel Boone's sons, Nathaniel and Daniel Morgan Boone, made salt for several years beginning about 1805. The Boone family had moved to Missouri from Kentucky with permission to settle the Femme Osage area, which was still under Spanish rule. They lived near present-day Defiance, which is also on the trail. More about the Boone's family history can be found in the section on **Defiance**.

The Missouri River Valley was a vital corridor that played a crucial part in the history and development of the West. Native Americans have sojourned along the Missouri River for thousands of years. The first wave of Europeans brought French trappers, traders and missionaries, who in the early 1700s followed the Mississippi River down from French Canada or up from French Louisiana, into the Missouri River Valley.

By the turn of the century, Americans from the Upper South had also penetrated the Missouri country, which was still under Spanish rule, to establish permanent settlements along the river at the Spanish government's behest. Daniel Boone was one of the first frontiersmen to forge ahead into this country.

A man by the name of Gottfried Duden also inspired the German migration and founding of many towns in the mid to late 1800s with his best-selling book in Germany that told of the Missouri River Valley's rich soils. The eastern end of the Katy Trail passes through this second "Rhineland" and is discussed in more detail in the **Dutzow** section, later in this book.

Many of the towns you will visit along the Katy Trail were subject to similar conditions. The Katy Trail route was established in the late 1890s. Once the Katy route was established, many new railroad villages were created. In Warren County, for example, Marthasville and Dutzow had long been in existence, but after the coming of the Katy, Peers and Treloar and several others were platted and named after St. Louis investors.

In the heyday of riverboat travel and the era of railroads, these towns prospered. They offered amenities from banks and newspapers to barber shops and lumber mills. As the main trade corridor moved up and out of the river bottoms to the asphalt interstate highways, many of these towns' populations and businesses declined or disappeared.

New Franklin is close to the original town of Franklin, where the Santa Fe Trail
began. New Franklin is "where the four trails meet" because the
Lewis and Clark Trail, the Katy Trail, the Santa Fe Trail
and the Boonslick Trail all pass through town.

New Franklin

Bikes • Camping • Food • Gas • Lodging • Parking • Post Office • Restrooms
Milepost 188
Milepost 191 at Old Franklin • Trail Mile Marker 189 at the Katy Roundhouse
3.6 miles across bridge from Boonville to New Franklin
9.9 miles from New Franklin to Rocheport
Boonville Chamber of Commerce for trail information: (816) 882-2721
or New Franklin City Hall: (816) 848-2288 • Zip Code: 65274

●●●●● CONNECTING ROUTE BETWEEN
FRANKLIN AND BOONVILLE TRAIL HEADS

From the Highway: From the I-70 Boonville exit,
take Route 5 north into New Franklin.

E a t s

Silver Liners Senior Center
On the square
(816) 848-2825

Katy Roundhouse
1983 Katy Drive
(816) 848-2232

Casey's General Store
Highway 5 & North Missouri
(816) 848-2212

L o d g i n g

Rivercene B&B
127 County Road 463
(816) 848-2497 or 1 (800) 531-0862
Rates: $80-130

Trails Inn
607 Clifton Heights
(816) 848-2776 or 848-2232
Rates: $55

C a m p g r o u n d s

Katy Roundhouse Deli, Convenience Store & Campground
1893 Katy Drive • (816) 848-2232

Take I-70 to Highway 5 to New Franklin. Turn left at the stoplight, then turn left
again at the carwash. **Note:** They also rent bikes and tents and have showers.

N ew Franklin is but a shadow of its past. The original town of Franklin,
located in the nearby river bottoms, was the scene of much activity for the
decade of its heyday in the early 1800s.

It was here in 1819 that the *Missouri Intelligencer and Boonslick Advertiser*,
the first newspaper west of St. Louis, began. That same year, the riverboat *Independence,* which was the first steamboat to successfully navigate the Missouri
River, docked in Franklin.

Franklin was also home to George Caleb Bingham, considered by many to be
the greatest American-born artist. The home in Arrow Rock where Bingham also
lived has been restored as part of a state historic site. Franklin was also home to
Kit Carson, who ran off from his apprenticeship to a saddlemaker with one of the
early overland trading expeditions to Santa Fe. It was the Santa Fe Trail opening in
1821, in fact, that marked the beginning of the real settlement of the Missouri
River Valley as well as the admission of Missouri to the Union as a state.

Unfortunately, a series of disastrous floods in the 1820s all but washed Franklin
away, which led to the construction of New Franklin on higher ground. Today
most activity in this area is concentrated in New Franklin. The current population
of New Franklin depends on which way you come into town. One end says 1,107;
the other 1,122.

Quilting has long been a fundraising activity at the Silver Liners Senior Center.
Quilters Elma Grotjan, left, Ester Wilmsmeyer, Anna Schumaker
and Kate Rohlfing have been quilting for "umpteen years."

A Common Thread

❖

Good food and great company tie the Silver Liners together

New Franklin's Main Street is a lonesome place at high noon. Most of the residents have already been drawn like magnets into the Silver Liners Senior Center, attracted by the lunch that can be had for a $2 donation.

The center has been feeding crowds of up to 70 people every afternoon, 5 days a week, for the last 17 years. Serving as the town's only restaurant is one way the center has been able to stay independent of state funding.

"It's such a hassle to do it their way," said Mary Harris, president of the Silver Liners. "You can't use any salt or fattening foods. This way we're free to do it our own way."

And "our way" means heaps of taco salad and a huge glass of sugared tea. Sour-cream squirters, sure to sound the cholesterol alarm, are within easy reach from any point along the two cafeteria-style tables. Most customers are regulars, here to eat and socialize. The center has drawn the community together through these afternoon meals and many other projects.

"Churches usually stage events within their own denomination," Harris said. "This center, though, gets us all together. Now I even forget who's Baptist."

On the first Sunday of each month, the center serves a $3.50 "all-you-can-eat" breakfast to more than 130 people. The smell of fresh sourdough biscuits, bacon, sausage and eggs greets visitors at the door.

"When the Katy Trail opened, many people would come out to ride it, and they'd eat breakfast here," Harris said.

In all, the center served more than 13,000 meals in 1993; half were carry-outs. Volunteers at the center deliver meals for those who can't get out.

"This is a valuable service to the community," Harris said. "Besides the food, it ensures that these people are being checked on each day. It does a lot of good."

The volunteers at the center take pride in helping the community and raising enough funds to stay independent.

"Although most senior centers are funded by the county, we decided to fund it ourselves," Harris said. "We bought the building and paid it off in two years with fundraisers."

The center continues to have pig roasts, Christmas bazaars, bake sales, card parties and special events for New Franklin's Santa Fe Days in September. About 125 members also pay $1 each for the privilege of being a Silver Liner.

The reason behind all of this work is to have a place they can call their own. Regulars gather every morning at the center to play cards and many stay to visit long after the noon dishes have been washed and dried.

The pace here is slow, marked more by the setting sun than any watch. The people here choose now to sit back and relax, savoring the peace and quiet that the center has to offer them.

If you are in New Franklin when the sun is high overhead and your stomach is feeling empty, stop in for the best lunch in town. And don't forget to say "please" and "thank you."

How to Get There: The Silver Liners Senior Center is located on the New Franklin Square. From the trail, take the road uphill to the carwash, take a right and go three blocks to the square. Silver Liners is on your left. From I-70, go to Highway 5, to New Franklin. At the stoplight, turn right and park. You're there. For more information, call (816) 848-2825.

Spiderwort

Katy Roundhouse:

Using diversity to blaze new business trails in Franklin

Business at the Katy Roundhouse in Franklin has been snowballing since their grand opening April 28, 1995. At the time, spring flooding had their leg of the Katy Trail trapped in on both sides, with only a mile of trail open on each side. Such a beginning would have caused an early fate for many a small business. But at the Roundhouse, business is booming thanks to John and Kim James' hard work, determination and the support of their family.

On this night, the restaurant is packed. Aside from her full-time job in Columbia, Kim serves as host and does the books. Mom is cooking up a storm in the kitchen and telling John incoming orders through an open window as he throws another filet mignon on the grill outside.

"And I also paint, scrub and decorate," Mom said through the window.

Diversity is a word John emphasizes when proffering advice for other would-be entrepreneurs. His advice: "not to totally depend on the trail. Have a backup."

"We have campgrounds, RV hookups, showers, a deli, bike rentals, homestyle dining and a wine and beer garden. Location is important. This place was sitting here waiting for us. You have to jump in and make things happen. Do your research. Offering something different — that's what we're shooting for. You have to be dedicated. I've been off my other job for a year, devoting all my time to this."

The James' attention to detail paid off. The authentic decor reminds diners they are in Franklin's old depot and switching station, where both John's grandfather and great-grandfather trod the woodend floors as Katy engineers.

"To see former railroad men and former Katy employees appreciate what you did with the place, it's the greatest reward. When you have a vision and follow through, and to see others appreciate it, that's what it's all about. Well, and making a little money along the way, of course."

Bikers from Chicago taking a break at the Katy Roundhouse.

Kinney's Folly Recalls Another Era

The Rivercene Bed and Breakfast, owned by Jody and Ron Lenz, was called Kinney's Folly by locals when an early riverboat captain decided to build it in the flood plain.

Capt. Joseph Kinney carried passengers from Montana to New Orleans with his fleet of 21 boats. On a single trip the *Cora No. 2* netted Capt. Kinney $50,000, which paid for the building of Rivercene.

For years he had collected building materials from all over the world — imported Italian marble for the nine fireplaces, black walnut for the front doors and hand-carved mahogany for the staircase. Construction began beside the river in 1864, despite warnings from settlers that the river would wash it away. He found the highest point the Missouri River had ever been and built the house one foot higher than that.

A few years after completion, the architecture was duplicated for the governor's mansion in Jefferson City. Capt. Kinney sold his last boat in 1882 when the railroads wrested away his business, and he died 10 years later. The home remained in the family until 1992, when it was purchased by Jody and Ron Lenz.

For 20 days during the flood of 1993, the Lenzes could reach Rivercene only by boat. The fully restored three-story mansion had four feet of river water dumped on its floor, costing its owners close to $200,000 in damages. After months of hard work, they reopened for business on January 1, 1994. Today the Rivercene once again glimmers with the regal air of Capt. Kinney's times.

How to Get There: Head north from Boonville across the Missouri River bridge and turn right on the first road (County Road 463). Rivercene is located a quarter mile east (on the left). Call (816) 848-2497 or 1 (800) 531-0862 for tours or more information.

Gratia and David Solomon of Colorado stop to read
one of Rocheport's many interpretive signs along the trail.

Rocheport

Bikes • Entertainment • Crafts • Food • Gas • Lodging
Parking • Post Office • Restrooms • Winery
Milepost 179
9.9 miles from New Franklin to Rocheport • 8.8 miles from Rocheport to McBaine
Trail Info: Trailside Café: (573) 698-2702 or Schoolhouse B&B: (573) 698-2022
For more information, call Friends of Rocheport: (573) 698-3595
Post Office, Second and Central: (573) 698-2605 • Zip Code: 65279

From the Highway: Rocheport is 12 miles west of Columbia, off of I-70. Take Exit 115 two miles north into town.

Eats

Flavors of the Heartland
next to the post office
204 Second Street
(573) 698-2063

Gregory House Antiques and Café Corner
off I-70 in Missouri River City
(573) 698-2919

Moniteau Creek Inn
next to the MKT Tunnel
(573) 698-2053

Trailside Café and Bike Rental
on the trail, near the train depot
1st and Pike • (573) 698-2702

Wilson's Texaco
off I-70 in Missouri River City
400 North Roby Farm Road
(573) 698-2058

Abigail's
on the trail, near the train depot
(573) 698-3000

Word of Mouth Café
near tunnel, next to post office
21 S. Central • (573) 698-2099

Lodging

Missouri River Inn
north of I-70
12800 Highway BB
(573) 698-2066

Roby River Run B&B • south of I-70
201 North Roby Farm Road
(573) 698-2173
Rates: $80-100

Schoolhouse B&B
Third and Clark
(573) 698-2022
Rates: $95-155

The Yates House B&B
305 2nd Street
(573) 698-2129
Rates: $95-105

Bicycle Rentals

Rocheport Cyclist
on the trail, near Abigail's
801 1st Street
(573) 698-2043

Trailside Café and Bike Rental
on the trail, near the train depot
1st and Pike
(573) 698-2707

Winery

Les Bourgeois Winery & Bistro
A-frame winery and a new full-course restaurant
On top of the bluff overlooking the Missouri River one mile from trail, Uphill
Highway BB & I-70 • (573) 698-2300

Rocheport

A s dusk approaches, Rocheport is a good place to be. As the locusts start to buzz at sundown, park the bike and let the occasional live performances at Moniteau Creek Outdoor Café carry you away.

Rocheport offers many amenities for the trail user and is a popular starting point for many Sunday saunterers. Here you'll find many historic homes, nationally renowned antique shops, craft shops, a vineyard, cafés and an 80-year-old schoolhouse restored into a bed and breakfast, which has garnered inclusion in a recent magazine's "Top 10 Most Romantic B&Bs in the U.S."

French for "port of rocks," Rocheport is better known today for its pleasant shopping district and historic flavor. With a population of 255, Rocheport entertains as many as 30,000 visitors each summer season, business owners estimate.

The local museum, (573) 698-7301, is an ideal place to recapture some of that early pioneer spirit. Open weekends from 1 p.m. to 4 p.m., it features artifacts and an extensive collection of black-and-white historical photographs.

The blackened ceiling of the Rocheport train tunnel is another reminder of the area's past. You can't say you've ridden the Katy Trail until you've passed through the MK&T tunnel, a 243-foot-long train tunnel built in 1893.

The tunnel has had a hard life. During the Flood of 1993, water in it stood four feet deep. A hundred years prior, in 1893, it was held hostage. McCormick Company, deciding they were underpaid, halted construction and placed 500 sticks of dynamite in the tunnel, threatening to blow it up if work resumed. After a three weeks standoff, sheriffs of Howard and Boone Counties overtook the bandidos. The tunnel was then completed by contractors Neal and O'Connell.

Photographs in the museum depict the arduous task of building Katy's only tunnel. It took 100 men and 40 teams of mules and horses four months to complete. Immigrants were quickly recruited by the railroad and paid a dollar a day.

The 1893
MK&T
Train Tunnel

Various nationalities of laborers followed the work, setting up "tent towns" at each site. Wardsville was closest to Rocheport. Zanzabar was of black immigrants, Dago City was comprised of Italians and Gillettsville was for the Irish.

The terrain reflects another important aspect of the area's history. The Moniteau bluffs near Rocheport are considered sacred by several tribes from the area. "Moniteau" is a French derivative of "Manitou," the Indian word for Great Spirit, hence the naming of Moniteau Creek.

The bluffs southeast of town bear a faded remnant of a Native American petroglyph. This is visible from the trail a few miles east of Rocheport above the Lewis and Clark cave (about mile 175), otherwise known as Torbett Spring. From the cave entrance (well marked by a Conservation sign) look 25-40 feet to the left and up approximately 35-50 feet. The maroon colored petroglyph of a "V" with a dot is right beside the bottom edge of the left bow of a prominent fracture impression. The crescent moon and dot symbol is thought to signify water, thus indicating the water source below for fellow travellers. The petroglyph appears to be the only one to survive the progress of man. The Lewis and Clark Expedition reported many "uncouth" murals and symbols upon the bluffs here, but couldn't examine them due to an infestation of rattlesnakes. Many were under overhanging bluffs that were summarily blasted off in later years to prevent train accidents.

Rocheport was also the site of the 1840 State Whig convention, where thousands gathered to support William Henry Harrison's presidential campaign. During the Civil War, Rocheport was raided by Confederate and Union troops alike.

Located on the Missouri River at the mouth of the Moniteau Creek, Rocheport grew rapidly as steamboat traffic increased. In 1849, 57 steamboats made 500 landings at Rocheport. That's more than one a day! During this age of accelerated growth, the area's trees were decimated. It was common for land owners to chop up wood, place it beside the river and post a price. Riverboats would pick up the wood, leave their price, and continue on.

Nathaniel Boone wrote that during his life, it took 13 men to girdle the average size tree in the Boonslick area. The passing of wagons was not a problem because even the lowest branches were still 20 feet above the ground.

Though fires in 1892 and 1922 destroyed many historic buildings, it was placed on the National Register of Historic Places in 1976. Historic walking tours are offered April through October by the Friends of Rocheport, (573) 698-3595.

Heading east, you're entering the Manitou Bluffs Region. Huge, white Burlington limestone bluffs flank the trail all the way to Jefferson City. These were formed as the skeletal remains of millions of sea creatures settled to the floor of ancient seas and were compressed under the massive weight of the ocean.

Nearby: Missouri River City, at the I-70 Rocheport Exit 115, has antique and gift shops plus an ice-cream parlor, a winery, a hotel and a play theater. Bikers should catch a ride up the 2-mile hill, which is steep, unrelenting and has no shoulder. The 275-million-year-old Boone Cave nearby may reopen soon.

The business district of Rocheport has antique stores, an art gallery, a volunteer fire department and a post office. A museum, cafés and a gift shop are also nearby.

Betty and Roger Slate opened the first business along the Katy.
Their business includes a café and bike rentals.

Trailside Café Fills Tall Orders for Bikers

The first business to be born along the trail was the Trailside Café in Rocheport, operated by Betty and Roger Slate. Starting with a sandwich shop in a single car garage, the Slates have worked tirelessly to build one of the best oases for bike riders on the trail.

"We almost never miss a day without a letter saying thanks for the hospitality," Betty said. Business has continued to expand, with Roger now handling numerous bike rentals while Betty tends to food preparation.

As I soon found out, busy sunny days are not such a good time to interview them for inclusion in the guidebook. As I began my barrage of questions "How many bikes? how much? how's business?" I realized that business was hopping and that a sunny afternoon was no time to be standing around answering questions on the meaning of life. What they needed was help. I put down my camera and grabbed a few bike rental forms and started handing them out to the people waiting to rent a bike. I dashed inside and asked Betty if she needed the help.

"You bet!" she said, busy behind the counter.

"Can you adjust this seat, mister?" and "Do you have a bike that would fit me?" type questions rained on my shoulders as I sought to get these visitors from Omaha, Nebraska, pedalling along our beautious trail.

Whether you're coming from Nebraska or next door, Trailside Café is a great place for a quick bite to eat, and for buying, renting and repairing bikes.

Campers' Note: Some group camping is allowed in Rocheport on a limited basis. Call (573) 698-2702 for more information, and see **Scout Outings Notes**.

Clark's Journal Entry Offers
Early Description of Rocheport Area

On May 14, 1804, the Lewis and Clark Expedition, called the "Corps of Discovery" left St. Louis and started up the Missouri River. Their mission, at the request of President Thomas Jefferson, was to explore the recently purchased Louisiana Territory.

The expedition passed near present-day Rocheport on June 7, 1804, and described the area of Moniteau Creek:

Set out early passed the head of the Island opposit which we Camped last night, and brackfast at the Mouth of a large Creek on the S.S. of 30 yds wide called big Monetou, from the pt. of the Isd. or Course of last night to the mouth of this Creek is N 61 degrees W, 4 1/2 ms. a Short distance above the mouth of this Creek, is Several Courious Paintings and Carveings in the projecting rock of Limestone inlade with white red and blue flint, of a verry good quality, the Indians have taken of this flint great quantities. We landed at this Inscription and found it a Den of rattle Snakes, we had not landed 3 minutes before three verry large Snakes wer observed on the Crevices of the rocks and Killed — at the mouth of the last mentioned Creek Capt. Lewis took four or five men and went to some Licks or Springs of Salt water from two to four miles up the Creek on Rt. side the water of those springs are not Strong, Say from 4 to 600 Gs. of water for a Bushel of Salt . . .

After reaching the Pacific Ocean, Lewis and Clark retraced their journey and passed Rocheport again on September 19, 1806.

Drawn and reproduced here courtesy of Martin Bellmann, from the book
Rocheport Memories, a project of the Friends of Rocheport and the Pen & Ink Club.

Native Americans were drawn by the Missouri River Valley's fertile soils
and abundant wildlife. They painted impressive images onto the limestone bluffs to signal important stops. The Moniteau bluffs near Rocheport
are particularly sacred.

Rocheport

In Good Faith — Expecting Nothing in Return
By Jan Parenteau

*I*n the summer of 1993, Rocheport survived its worst flood. This essay is in awe *and gratitude to the many thousands of people who came to help; who through sheer will and muscle power saved the town. Despite the heat, humidity and physical intensity involved in building sandbag levees, no one had a heart attack or even fainted. The most wonderful part were these volunteers who "came in good faith, expecting nothing in return."*

What follows is a letter I wrote to my son who was stationed in Saudi Arabia during the period of the impending Gulf War . . .

Sunday morning, August 1, 1993
Hot and very humid
No longer "Waiting for Noah"

Dear David,

The Missouri River began cresting early Thursday morning, much sooner than expected. Flood waters are four feet higher than they were at the height of the July 15th flood. It's been hard to sleep. Despite physical exhaustion, I am pried awake by the sound of the rushing, angry river, and the hum of dozens of pumps trying to keep water away from homes surrounded by levees built by hundreds of volunteers.

Through some sort of miracle, we lost electricity for only 14 hours, when the levee was breached near the power substation at Little Bonne Femme. The water came surging in so fast it broke both poles and power lines. Swift current prevented the necessary repairs. Lucky for us, a patched-in system with an adjoining county put us back on the grid.

My efforts have been minor compared to the extended hours, day after day, put in by many of the people who live here. Still, I have done everything from filling sandbags to throwing them, from turning bags (they arrive inside out and must be reversed before filling) to serving food. Throwing sandbags is difficult — they can weigh from 25 to 60 pounds, depending on who filled them and whether they are wet.

"Piece of cake!" The young man in line next to me would shout. I knew it would be one of the lighter ones. But when he yelled "dead gorilla," I knew to brace myself. Unfortunately, my old body didn't hold up too long and I soon had to give way to younger and stronger men and women. There were many such folk, but I think most often of my neighbor, Lela. Tall, slender and strong, a true pioneer woman, she was everywhere, working as hard or harder than most men. Many others spent hours making food, cleaning, serving, turning or filling sandbags. The most miraculous of all were the deskbound men and women, from all walks of life, who came to Rocheport and dared the blazing sun and relentless humidity, to work hour after hour on the snake-like levee which protected the town.

Turning sandbags is easier than tossing them. Still, there is an intensity to it and your hands and arms get sore from the roughness. People, mostly women, but some men, sit in a circle in or around the fire station, which is the hub of all flood activity, and talk about the enormity of the event taking place before their eyes.

Inside the station, the Salvation Army rushes about nonstop, preparing food and thousands of drinks for the workers. This group from Flint, Michigan, more than 800 miles away, is a wonder to watch. They do an incredible job of taking mountains of assorted donated food and making it into decent meals, and they do it all with jokes and smiles.

Before I know it, break is over and I return to the Ballew's home, surrounded by an enormous sandbag levee. It holds most of the water outside and gasoline pumps help take care of the rest. You have to use a rowboat to get to it. They have been sleeping on the floor of the house so that if a pump goes off they will know right away. They have moved everything out just in case the unthinkable happens.

On Wednesday night the National Guard rolled in. They brought bigger pumps and people who were rested and able to take charge. Most of the Rocheport Volunteer Fire Department, which hadn't slept for days, went home and collapsed. No one had really known exactly what to do, for this situation had never existed before. As one fireman expressed it, "We went from amateurs to pros with no experience in-between."

The break is bad and the water is gushing in —
people have to sit on the bags to hold them in place
until the next one goes on top . . .

When I came home from work on Thursday, there was a National Guard roadblock at the only road left open into town. Hundreds of volunteers had been coming in to help, plus almost as many tourists, who seemed to view the action around the flood much as they would a TV show, uninvolved. They were often in the way of the real work. At this point, it was made clear no one could come into Rocheport unless they lived here or were dressed like they were going to sandbag.

How can I explain to you the emotional roller coaster the whole town was on? Picture this: It is 4:30 a.m, on Thursday. Some of the volunteers are coming off night shift and grabbing a bite to eat at the fire station. Everyone is exhausted and worried; the river is still rising and in places very close to topping the sandbag levee. According to the Corps of Engineers, it may be another 24 to 48 hours to crest. Ross Perot is due into town and there are some jokes about whether the volunteers should go home and clean up — after all, they want to make a good impression if they appear on national TV. At that moment, a woman comes running down the street yelling, "The levee's breaking by my house." The volunteers take off running. A fireman quickly sounds the alarm and hurries after them.

Rocheport

The break is bad and the water is gushing in — people have to sit on the bags to hold them in place until the next one goes on top. Some dive for the bags which are escaping into the swift current. Other people join in. Everyone is working feverishly. Gradually, the break is closed. Victory! There are grins, slapping of wet clothes in the moist dawn air. "Still gonna go home and shower for TV?" One of the volunteers teases a fireman. "Heck no," he answers, "haven't got time." Much to everyone's relief, that morning was the beginning of the crest.

By Saturday there's a line of debris and wet on the street where water had stood the day before. Also, the top of the park's basketball hoop has reappeared. Already the stench of rotting fish, vegetation and sewage permeates the town. The river is full of logs, propane tanks, debris, even coffins, deliberate dumps of chemicals and other hazardous wastes, snakes, water beetles and leeches. If those don't bother you, there are chiggers, biting flies, relentless sun and humidity.

We received a call at 3:30 a.m. from some reporter in New Zealand who wanted us to photograph our house! He seemed undaunted by the fact that we lived on a hill.

Well, Ross Perot did visit here and national morning show host, Harry Smith, plus numerous other celebrities both major and minor. We, for example, received a call at 3:30 a.m. from some reporter in New Zealand who wanted us to photograph our house! He seemed undaunted by the fact that we lived on a hill. The mayor is being overwhelmed by calls from the media, too, both national and international.

Ironically, at this point, the only foreign country to offer us flood relief aid was the poor third world country of Bangladesh. Ross Perot's public relation people were right. Rocheport was the place to come to talk to the American people about the flood. The citizens of Rocheport working with others in facing this catastrophe have given me back my faith in the grit and fortitude of the American people to pull together in difficult times. This, then, is the silver lining of this awful event.

Love,

Mom

Postscript: Saudi Arabia. Late August 1993.

My son, David, was so taken with this letter that he went to a very grim U.N. guard from Bangladesh who patrolled a nearby airstrip and told him thank you for the offer of help from his country — that both he and his mother appreciated it. For the first time since David arrived, the guard spoke to him. "We understand about floods," he said simply. The two men smiled at one another in the hot desert sun and in that moment, half a world away, the Mighty Mo became a diplomat.

Large bluffs line the
trail from Rocheport to
Jefferson City.

Marge McDermott and Marti Kardinal explore dog-propulsion along the Katy.

Rocheport

Pepper began his walk across the United States in Olympia, Washington.

One Veteran's Sojourn of Sorrow

Holding his breath and a billowing Old Glory at half-mast, Frederick Pepper edged his way across the I-70 Missouri River Bridge as semitrailers made those 200 tons of steel and concrete shiver.

Pepper, 45, arrived in Missouri after carrying his flag, a message and little else, all the way from Olympia, Washington.

"We lower our flags to half-mast when we are mourning a loss," Pepper said. "My flag is at half-mast because I am mourning the sad state of our heroes. The American people are not aware of the facts concerning our nation's vets."

According to Pepper, 40 percent of all homeless people in the United States are military veterans. Pepper said budget cuts have limited access to proper medical treatment for low-income veterans even as veterans and their families battle the much-debated Persian Gulf syndrome, and side effects from the exposure to Agent Orange. According to Pepper, Persian Gulf syndrome was caused by exposure to radioactive contamination.

"Our children are being born bent and crooked and our nation is not providing even the minimum assistance," he said. "Veterans Affairs gobbles up the budget with administrative costs. It's like we own the store but got so busy paying taxes on it that it doesn't work anymore."

Pepper began his journey on June 21, 1995. He has accepted a few rides but the purpose of his trip isn't to hitchhike. He plans to walk to Washington, D.C., carrying his message and his flag, at half-mast, the whole way.

Pepper intends to arrive in Washington, D.C., on Veterans Day, November 11, to urge policy makers to reconsider benefit funding for veterans. Pepper is an honorably discharged Vietnam Veteran, who served in the U.S. Navy from 1969-1973. Pepper has been an advocate for veterans affairs for much of his life in Washington state. He is also a cofounder of a Washington-area veterans homeless program.

"Congress cut $7.6 billion out of the Veteran Administration medical budget and if you've seen the movie *Fourth of July*, you know exactly what they're doing to our heroes."

"Do you think walking across America is a good way to get people to hear your message?" the reporter asked.

"I'm talkin' to you, aren't I?" he said with a smile. "We live in a country of people who recycle their trash but then let their heroes sleep under bridges. Heroes deserve someone to do this for them. Heroes aren't of the nature to cry and whine. I'm doing what I can to reawaken the American people to the plight of the veterans. I just want to make it right."

Walking alongside the surging steel of interstates, Pepper stands out as a cultural and visual anachronism. He was arrested for walking along the highway in Topeka, Kansas, and spent three days in jail. But his experience has largely been a positive one.

"People have really helped me get my gear up the road. People have offered food and a place to stay at night. The Baptist Church in Concordia, Missouri, took me to church Sunday."

Pepper says faith in his mission and in God has kept him moving forward. Frequent calls home for encouragement from his wife and children also lengthen his strides toward D.C.

"I eat when I'm hungry. I sleep when I'm tired. You learn to go without, out here. I started this trip weighing 200 pounds. I'm down to 170. I didn't need that extra weight."

According to Pepper, many people have likened his journey to that of the dim-witted movie character Forrest Gump. Time to think upon a thousand dusty roads has perfected his response to this comparison: "He ran. I walk. Forrest had a four-year education. I went to a two-year. He's a lot more patient and Tom Hanks is better looking."

From the truckers' horn blasts as Pepper salutes passersby, it seems the patriotic enthusiasm generated by his flag-waving will take him to D.C. if nothing else.

Barbara Hofstetter, Katy Trail State Park ranger, talks to biker David Misslin
on the Perche Creek bridge. As you cross the bridge, take note
of the high-water marks about a foot above your head.

McBaine

Food • Parking • Picnic Table • Restrooms • Water
Milepost 169
8.8 miles from Rocheport to McBaine • 7 miles from McBaine to Easley
10 miles to Columbia along the MKT Bicycle Trail spur
Call Betty's Grill for trail information: (573) 445-6899
Zip Code: 65203

From the Highway: From Columbia,
take Providence Road south to Route 163 to Route K.

Eats

Betty's Bar and Grill
7155 West Route K • (573) 445-6899
Mon.-Sat. 8 a.m. - 9 p.m., Sun. 11 a.m. - dark

In September of 1899, the first locomotive reached Columbia on the MKT rail line that connected to the Katy here in McBaine. At this junction, the "frontier town" of McBaine grew out of a cornfield, 5,000 acres of bluegrass and the aspirations of a world-class cattleman named Turner McBaine.

For years, there were merely a flag station and Gilvin's grocery store. Turner McBaine realized the economic potential of this junction point, plotted the town of McBaine and auctioned off lots on September 20, 1899, only two weeks after the branch began operation.

But the railroad saw McBaine as merely a convenient switching station. Passengers could hop on a train in Columbia at night, sleep until their car was switched to the eastbound Katy Flyer in McBaine and greet the morning in St. Louis without waking.

The MKT Columbia branch of the railroad turned into the MKT Fitness Trail around 1983 after lying dormant for 10 years. This bicycle trail connects riders to Forum Boulevard in Columbia. The juncture for this trail is 100 feet (west) of the Perche Creek railroad bridge in McBaine.

This trail, developed cooperatively by the city of Columbia and Boone County, is 8.9 miles long. It officially opened to McBaine in October 1996. It is now marked with a "Hindman Junction" sign, honoring Columbia Mayor Darwin Hindman, president of the Katy Trail Coalition, for the role he played in supporting development of the Katy Trail.

Betty Moss, owner of Betty's Grill and Tavern, takes a break with
co-worker Rachael Kendall before the dinner rush. She is the
only McBaine business owner who rebuilt after the floods.

UNYIELDING

Betty Moss isn't your typical woman. But then again, McBaine isn't your typical town.

McBaine was all but washed away during the flood of 1993. After the flood, only two of the 35 residents stubbornly remained. Today Betty counts the town residents at "6 people and 6 dogs."

Moss ran the Hideaway Bar and Grill in the McBaine river bottoms for eight years, until the building was gutted by the flood. "I rebuilt here because it's home," she said. "My life was in that restaurant."

Many McBaine residents moved away to rebuild on higher ground, tired of the uncertainties of living in the flood plain. Moss stubbornly refused.

Today, her new white three-story structure towers over the remains of the flood-ravaged town. And business is "real good," she said, but "there's a few stragglers that say 'I didn't know you were open.'"

Moss serves a curious bunch in her new restaurant. Customers in mud-caked boots and Italian cycling shoes all find space along the varnished countertop to eat lunch or pass the afternoon. Her location right off the Katy Trail has given her a chance to meet riders who stop in expressly for her cheeseburgers.

The new building was built over the remnants of her last restaurant. When standing flood waters receded after three weeks, all that remained were three feet of mud and the saturated hull of her old building. The flood tore all the fixtures and walls apart and took the roof off.

"We had to bulldoze it. We had a lot of good times in that old place," Moss said. "It was great . . . ugly, but great. It was just one big old room with a juke box and a pool table and the bar," she said. One wall was covered with graffiti. A tradition was to write your name on the wall when you visited. "There were pictures from all the years I've been down here — parties and fish fries. The kids really liked it."

Moss was even flooded out again while rebuilding. "It's still a mess," she said, "but all you can do is plod along." The new structure is built on seven-foot-high risers to keep the restaurant up out of subsequent flood waters, if the need arises (pardon the pun). The Missouri River is two miles to the west and Betty's is well out of the 100-year flood plain, "but they were calling the 1993 flood a 500-year flood," Moss said. "I don't plan on being around for the next one."

"Floods are a way of life down here," Moss says. Her building is located only 100 yards from Perche Creek, which floods McBaine almost annually as it drains Columbia's spring rain runoff. Sometimes the restaurant is only reachable by boat, with three to four feet of water in every direction for 300 feet. Because her home is upstairs, the flood waters do little to alter the ebb and flow of Moss's daily life. When there's water, "they all come by boat to eat and check in on me," she says.

Betty's has a pool table, restrooms and **cold water near the door for bikers.** Her food selections range from fantastic chili dogs and hamburgers to $7.95 prime rib specials on Thursday nights. She usually also has a lunch special.

How to Get There: Go south of the Katy Trail in McBaine to the huge white restaurant. By car, take I-70 to Columbia's Providence Road Exit, follow it south 'til you reach McBaine. If you end up in the river, you've gone too far. Call (573) 445-6899 for more information.

Betty's Grill and Tavern in McBaine.

McBAIN

To 'E' Or Not To 'E'?

A sign welcoming drivers to McBaine has raised the attention of passersby.
By Michael J. Hamtil

❖

Someone forgot something in McBaine.

That something is its name — or at least the last letter.

The residents of this quiet river bottom town never seemed to mind that the "e" at the end of McBaine was silent, but they certainly noticed when it turned up missing on the sign.

The misspelled sign has been on the shoulder of Route K just east of the Katy Trail displaying six-sevenths of the town's name for almost three months.

"It's definitely wrong on the sign," McBaine town clerk Lucille Coleman said. "It's supposed to be 'M-C-B-A-I-N-E.' I don't know who put that up there, but they can't even get the name of our town right."

Kim Miranda, of the transportation department, said this kind of thing has happened before. Although she can't say exactly what happened to the missing "e," she said human error is probably to blame.

"Well, one person cuts out the letters, and one applies them to the board." Miranda said. "So either someone failed to cut out the 'e,' or someone failed to put it on."

On the other hand, someone could have spelled the name of the town wrong at some time during the ordering process. "It goes through half-a-dozen hands before it's done, and it must have gotten changed somewhere along the line," she said.

So how do the residents feel about the mistake?

"Well, I don't think it will be too hard to change," Mayor Marvin Sapp said. "But of course, it will probably cost $200 for the paperwork and 20 cents for the letter."

In a town such as McBaine, things like street signs don't appear to mean much. Take Stanley Baker, for example. "I always thought I lived on Stone Street," he said. "But just the other day, Marvin (Sapp) pointed out to me that I actually live on Katy.'

The same is true for Dale Roberts, a 44-year resident. "Hell, I been through too many floods. This kind of thing doesn't bother me none. And the signs, people just run them over and knock them down anyway," he said. Coleman plans on calling the highway department to get the misspelling taken care of sooner or later.

McBaine residents know who they are, and "e" or no "e," for them, their town will always have a happy ending.

Reprinted from the *Columbia Missourian*, July 4, 1994

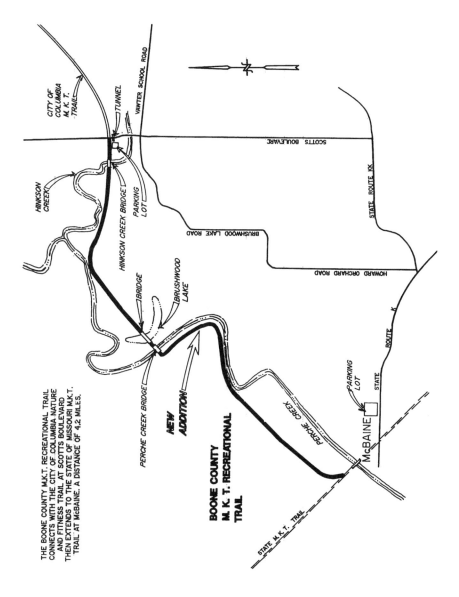

THE BOONE COUNTY M.K.T. RECREATIONAL TRAIL CONNECTS WITH THE CITY OF COLUMBIA NATURE AND FITNESS TRAIL AT SCOTTS BOULEVARD THEN EXTENDS TO THE STATE OF MISSOURI M.K.T. TRAIL AT McBAINE, A DISTANCE OF 4.2 MILES.

Map of MKT Fitness Trail Spur to Columbia

The MKT Fitness Trail goes from McBaine to Columbia, passes a swimming lake with sand beaches and leads directly into the heart of Columbia. Distance from McBaine to Columbia is 8.9 miles, which normally takes about one hour to ride. Look for the "Hindman Junction" sign just west of the railroad bridge in McBaine.

Mike Akers and his son Michael enjoy a spring sunset near the Great Burr Oak. This 350-year-old, 84-foot-high tree has been in the Williamson family for six generations.

The Great Burr Oak Tree of Mid-Missouri

The lush green crown of leaves spans 106 feet, providing shade for travellers along the gravel road between the Katy Trail and the cornfields. It's the first thing you see when you come around the bend.

The 350-year-old landmark has survived it all — the tests of time, lightning strikes and the Great Flood of '93, even though water lapped at its limbs 8 feet above the ground.

It is the State Champion Burr Oak tree. And to six generations of John Sam Williamson Jr.'s family who owns the land under the burr oak, it is the "big old tree that refuses to die."

But last year, Williamson discovered the enormous trunk covered with bright spray paint and carvings.

"How could somebody do that to the tree after it has survived so much?" he asked, as he pointed out scars from the several lightning strikes the tree has survived.

The tree had been vandalized before but never to this extent. While the vandalism is ugly, it's not really a danger to the tree's life. The paint will have to remain because trying to peel or chemically remove the paint would hurt the tree worse. It may take three years to wear off.

Three years is not long for the oak, which is expected to live 100 years more. But to Williamson, the saddest part about the vandalism is that people will no longer be able to enjoy the tree.

"It's not unusual to see couples looking at the tree or having a picnic," he said. "One time, there was a fellow down here playing the drums, with a whole trap set. He said he was going to play while the sun went down.

"As far as the scheme of things, this is not as bad as a life-threatening crime," said Williamson. "It is just a sad thing that people want to deface the tree."

❖

How to Get There: When travelling the Katy Trail from Rocheport to McBaine, once you cross the Perche Creek bridge in McBaine, you'll take the first (and only) street south into town. Follow this road past Betty's Restaurant and over the levee. It'll wind around for close to a mile and you'll soon see the Great Burr Oak, beside a smaller 200-year-old tree. **Or**, from Huntsdale, at the junction of Grocery Branch and Coats Lane, hang a right and the tree is less than half a mile.

Pebble Publishing just finished cleaning up the place and repainting the concrete marker. Please do your part by respecting the adjacent farmers' fields.

Columbia

Bikes • Entertainment • Food • Gas • Lodging
Microbrewery • Post Office • Restrooms • RV Park
Off the trail • 10 miles north of McBaine
Accessible via the MKT Fitness Trail
Columbia Convention and Visitors Bureau: (573) 875-1231
Chamber of Commerce: (573) 874-1132
Post Office: (573) 876-7829 • Zip Codes: 65201, 65202, 65203, 65205
From the Highway: Located on I-70
midway between St. Louis and Kansas City.

Bike Shops

Birdsong Bicycle Repair
315 N. Eighth Street
(573) 815-9960

Cycle Extreme
915 Cherry Street
(573) 874-7044
and
2101 W. Broadway
(573) 446-1978

Jim's Bike Shop
1002 N. Old Highway 63
(573) 442-7011

Tryathletics
1 S. Fourth Street
(573) 443-8875

Walts Bicycle and Fitness Shop
1217 Rogers Street
(573) 886-9258

Bed & Breakfasts

Teddy Bear's Bed & Breakfast
3201 Brown Station Road
(573) 474-1613 and 474-7477
Rates: $50

University Avenue Bed & Breakfast
1315 University Avenue
(800) 499-1920 and (573) 499-1920
Rates: $75

R V P a r k

Cottonwoods RV Park
3 miles north of I-70 on Highway 63
Full hook-ups, restrooms, showers and laundromat
5170 N. Oakland Gravel Road
(573) 474-2747

Columbia is probably best known for Tiger Football. The University of Missouri has allowed this town of 80,000 to grow more quickly than its neighbors.

Located midway between Kansas City and St. Louis along Interstate 70, Columbia is quietly turning from town to city. Growth in the last few years has continually surpassed 6 percent, which is twice the national average. *Money Magazine* has consistently rated Columbia as one of the best places to live in the U.S., becoming only one of two cities to appear among the top 20 places to live in four straight years.

Columbia is accessible directly off the Katy Trail by heading north from McBaine on the MKT Fitness Trail. This tree-lined route takes you by several lakes and sneaks you through suburbia into the heart of Columbia. There are numerous bike shops in town if you're needing a rim straightened and Columbia has every amenity common to a town this size, including 23 hotels. Of particular note to Katy Trail aficionados is the Katy Station Restaurant, located at 402 E. Broadway, (573) 449-0835. This is the old train depot, which has been renovated into a fine restaurant, complete with many old photographs of the Katy and early memorabilia.

As you ride this part of the trail, keep one eye skyward for the many hot-air balloons that will be dotting the summer sky in August. Some 250,000 people are expected to converge on Columbia for the U.S. Hot Air Balloon Championships. Call the Visitors Bureau, the Chamber of Commerce or the Balloon Nationals Info Hotline, (573) 446-5566, for more information.

There is also a 24-hour hotline, (573) 443-2222, for information on entertainment and activities in and around Columbia. For a listing of all the summer's hot-air balloon events, look for the *Columbia Business Times'* Balloon Chasers Guide.

LOCAL FARMERS LET YOU
TAKE YOUR PICK

❖

So you say you want some fresh fruits and vegetables? Why not head straight to the source and give local orchards and fresh food markets a try? Here is a partial list to get you fed. Many of the dealers even allow you to pick your own. Please call before you go. For a complete listing, contact the Missouri Department of Agriculture, at (573) 875-5291.

Alexander's Farm Market
4601 South Brushwood Lake Road • (573) 445-1491
(Seven miles west on I-70 to Exit 117)
Apples, peaches, pecans, cantaloupe, pumpkins, corn, tomatoes and watermelon.
Open: July through November, seven days a week, noon - 5 p.m.

Chuck Basye Farms
15001 West Highway 40, Rocheport • (573) 698-2906
Pick-your-own blackberries, various vegetables, cantaloupe, pumpkins, watermelon and tomatoes.
Open: June through October, Fri.-Tues. 11 a.m. - dusk

Fletcher's Greenhouse & Orchard
4280 Highway 763 North, Columbia • (573) 449-4397
Green beans, cantaloupe, peaches, pumpkins, watermelon, tomatoes and squash.
Open: March through Christmas, Mon.-Sat. 9 a.m. - 5:30 p.m., Sun. noon - 5 p.m.

Prairie Wind Farm
Rt. 2 Box 185, Centralia • (573) 682-1562
(Farm is located six miles north of Centralia on Route C)
Blueberries and blackberries.
Open: mid-June through first frost.

The Red Barn (Valley View Orchard)
3602 Christian School Road, Hartsburg • (573) 657-9522
(Three miles north of Hartsburg up Jemerson Road)
Large variety of fruits, vegetables, and berries including apples, cherries, eggplant, squash, tomatoes.
Open: March 30 through December 25, all week 10 a.m. - 6 p.m.

S.G.B. Farms
725 East Cedar Tree Lane, Hartsburg • (573) 657-2989
(Highway 63 to Ashland, seven miles west on Route M, left on Cedar Tree)
Pick-your-own blueberries.
Open: June 15 through mid-July, Thur.-Sat. 11 a.m. - dark. Please call first.

Sunny Acres Organic Farm
1750 South Rangeline, Columbia • (573) 442-9324
Pick-your-own: large variety of vegetables including asparagus, broccoli, peppers, potatoes, cucumbers and watermelon.
Open: May through September, Mon.-Fri., 5 p.m. - dark, Sat., dawn - dusk

Easley

• Parking •
Milepost 162
7 miles from McBaine to Easley • 5.1 miles from Easley to Wilton
From the Highway: From I-70, take Providence exit (Columbia)
south to 163 then take Route N.

E asley's the kind of place you could zip right through and feel like you didn't miss a thing. There isn't much man-made here to distract you from the greater pastime of enjoying nature.

You may not notice much if you ride into town, but to drive in on the winding road down into the bottoms, the air actually smells sweeter once you get down here. Have a seat and soak it in.

The bluffs here are some of the tallest on the trail and continue to keep you company until you get to Hartsburg. Easley's Store was rebuilt after the flood, and owner Mike Gamble says he is planning to reopen . . . someday . . . maybe.

People throwing iron horseshoes while clad in biker's spandex isn't the first picture that comes to mind when someone mentions the U.S. Coast Guard. But here along the Missouri, you may run across one of the Guard's crews frequenting the trail for a little "R&R" wherever they dock up for the night.

"We ride the trail wherever we end up for the night — St. Charles, Mokane, Hermann, Easley . . . we like to stop and ride whenever we get a chance," said Chief Engineer Don Deede (pictured above) between throwing horseshoes.

"We hop on our morale bikes and go for a ride," said one crewman.

On your whats?

"The Coast Guard calls them morale bikes. One day we rode from Easley to Rocheport and back in one day."

The 13-person crew cruises the river on trips that last from 14 to 20 days, placing buoys to warn boats of possible snags. They patrol from the mouth at St. Louis to Kansas City. Because they can only work during daylight, they often tie their tug up by the nearest town and hop on their bikes for a short ride before sundown.

"When I joined the Coast Guard, I didn't think it'd be anything like this," a crewman said.

The U.S. Coast Guard places buoys in the Missouri to prevent tugs from snagging. In the 1800s, dangerous snags on this river prevented river boats' lifespans from stretching more than one or two seasons.

Birds of the same feather . . . Michael Cooper and his love birds.

Cooper's Landing
By R. C. Adams

❖

Katy Trail Hiker Hint No. 23-C: If your water bottle's run dry, if a roofer's nail has impailed your bike's back tire, or if you're just a little lost outside of Easley, Missouri — you'll be in luck when you find the eclectic, multipurpose Cooper's Landing.

"I'm pretty much open anytime I'm here," owner Michael Cooper says. Armed with a desire to leave the nine-to-five, time-clock way of life, Cooper's entrepreneurial efforts along the MKT trail began simply with a tackle shop and concession booth in March of '92. Since the Flood of '93, he's diversified considerably.

Today Cooper still sells worms and lures, sodas, snacks and beer, but he also offers hikers, bikers, and boaters a small campground, a boat club, a small engine repair shop — even a local music haven and a small-scale aviary.

All of these endeavors occur in and around Cooper's two-story home and business. Cooper's Landing is tucked between the MKT Trail and the Missouri River on one acre just west of Easley.

A vision of such an environment started getting pretty clear to Cooper nearly a decade ago, soon after he had moved "down to the river" from Columbia. Although he continued to commute to Columbia to work for several years, eventually the opportunity arose for Cooper to start his own business.

"I wanted something that would be fun, but not terribly demanding," he says. After three years of running a store out of the lower level of his home, Cooper's hoping the summers will see a return to the way things were before the flood — even better, as the MKT grows.

Financially, Cooper says the Flood still affects how much he can invest in the growth of his business. But for most facets of his business, the overhead is pretty low and the return relatively quick. Another reason for this season's optimism, he says, is that a lot of the repairs were handled last year.

On weekends and late afternoons he stays at the store. Occasionally friends spell him for a few hours. A few friends have become business partners of sorts with certain aspects of the business.

Selling hand-fed love birds and parakeets, for example, takes a lot of work and knowledge, Cooper says. One friend breeds the birds and brings the babies to Cooper for several weeks of hand-feeding. Cooper says a hand-fed love bird currently sells for $60.

"They all have a unique personality," Cooper says, looking at a few permanent members of his flock. "People say they have the intelligence of a three-year-old and the maturity of a two-year-old."

The Easley music scene is something Cooper is particularly interested in nurturing. It involves many of his friends. Already there have been informal acoustic jam sessions on Saturday afternoons around a fire on the campground. He says anyone can bring a guitar or harmonica and get to know other people.

Cooper would like to host bands on Saturday nights, either travelling groups or bands formed from the Saturday afternoon jam sessions.

On Mondays, the landing is closed, in principle, though travellers often find a way to open the business briefly. "People come here, see the sign saying 'closed,' then ring the bell,' which is just fine when they need help," Cooper says. "People get stranded out here all the time."

Cooper's personal river ferry is a 14-foot runabout, an army-green aluminum Studebaker. It's been with him since he came to the river. Like most other boats that join the Cooper's Landing Boating Club, Cooper's Studebaker has been thoroughly seasoned by the Missouri River. "We try to do our boating upstream," Cooper says, "so if something breaks down, we can get back."

To buy a love bird, join the boat club or work out a gig for your band on Saturday night, give Michael Cooper a call at (573) 657-2544.

Campers' Note: If you're looking for a great view of the river, Cooper's place can't be beat. It's RIGHT on the river. Camping is primitive, with water, a bathroom and shower. The pay phone's number out front is (573) 657-9301. This is a great place for eagle watching.

Wilton

As part of a Valentine's Day tradition, Pastor Elder Marvine Tolle (center) and the other men of the Goshen Primitive Baptist Church in Wilton prepare an elaborate dinner and serve it to the women of the community.

Wilton

Crafts • Food • Parking
5.1 miles from Easley to Wilton
3.8 miles from Wilton to Hartsburg

From the highway: Wilton can be reached by taking the river road either south from Easley or north from Hartsburg. Or, take I-70 to 63 South (at Columbia) heading to Jefferson City and take the Ashland exit to the right. Stay on Route M (blacktop) until you reach the river.

Eats

Riverview Traders Restaurant & General Store
Right across from the trail
18300 River Road
(573) 657-1095

Campground & River Cruises

Primitive camping and tipi camping may become available soon. Sunset river cruises are also available. Call the Riverview Traders Store for more information and reservations.

By far the biggest commotion to occur in Wilton on most days is the chorus that begins at the first crimson light of dusk, as flocks of birds alight in the area's large oaks to enjoy nature's salutorial display at the end of each day.

The quiet ebb and flow of life here make it the perfect perch. This small town could soon be quite a haven for trail users as well. The ambitious drive of several residents seems to be leading a revival in the truest sense for this tiny river bottom community.

In addition to the general store and restaurant, camping and limited river-shuttle service may become available in Wilton during the 1997 season.

"Accommodations will initially be primitive, but we hope to have cooking and improved bathing facilities by mid to late season," Robert Riesenmy said.

The Riesenmys, who own the Riverview Traders Store in Wilton, express their Native American heritage throughout their store. The store is impossible to miss if you keep an eye out for the house directly across the trail with several tipis in the yard.

In addition to food and groceries, the Riesenmy shop is overflowing with crafts, Plains and Woodland Indian tribe artwork and paintings. The couple also sell hand-crafted tipis. Retreats and private workshops are also available.

In a joint venture with neighbor William Duvall, they are planning to offer limited river-shuttle service. "We hope to start picking up biking groups in Jefferson City, for example, and shuttling them up to Rocheport or beyond for a leisurely ride back home," Robert said. Since service is limited, call (573) 657-1095 for more information. Dates must be set in advance.

Bikers' Note: One mile east of Wilton is the Wilton Boat Club's shelter and boat ramp. There's a shelter, picnic tables and electricity. A Corps of Engineers river buoy is also visible from this outlook. These are placed to mark the channel. There's almost always a cool breeze and a bit of shade at these picnic tables.

Maggie and Robert Riesenmy sell tipis and Native American crafts at their store in Wilton.

Wilton

Robert keeps his Osage traditions alive in many ways. Here he is dressed in full Osage regalia to dance at an area pow wow.

A silent reminder of Wilton's pioneering past, this log cabin is one of dozens that dot the countryside along the trail.

Berries Can Pull You Out of a Blue Funk

By E. Crystal Cornell

❖

C. L. Scrivner and Alleen Scrivner give suggestions
for picking and storing blueberries.

Blueberries won't be ripe until mid-June, but it's never too early to re-fresh your basics on blueberry picking, storage and cooking.

"Ripe blueberries should just roll off the branch," said Alleen Scrivner. "If they are a little pink, they're not ripe. If you have to pull them off the branch, they're not ready."

The Scrivners own a blueberry farm in Hartsburg, where you can come to pick your own berries and pay by the pound. After your berries are picked, they offer some advice for berry care and storage.

Unripe berries won't be as sweet and the quality won't be as good, said C. L. Scrivner. "Unripe berries have a sugar content of 11 or 12 percent. If you wait until they're dead ripe, they'll go up to 14 to 16 percent sugar," he said.

If you want to use your berries all year round, put them in the freezer but don't rinse them, Alleen Scrivner said. They'll freeze separately like marbles, and you can measure out as much as you need.

"Don't wash them until you're ready to use them," she said. "If you wash them (before freezing), they'll get wet and be a big blob of blueberries."

The Scrivners caution that if you want to store your berries in the fridge in-stead of the freezer, you still must rinse them just before you need to use them or they will get soft and moldy. "If you want to eat them fresh, they'll keep for one to two weeks in the fridge," Alleen Scrivner said.

The Scrivners use their berries to make their own blueberry wine and other blueberry products such as cakes, jams and sauces. However, they also borrow many ideas from outside sources. "Anytime I see something in a magazine I think would be good, that's what I try," she said.

To get to SGB Farms at 725 East Cedar Tree Lane, take U.S. 63 to Ashland. Go west on Route M 7.2 miles to Wilton. Turn west on Cedar Tree Lane and go one mile. The farm is on the left, and the Scrivner mailbox is on the right.

However, don't get yourself in a dither to go berry hunting until mid-April, when blueberries are in full bloom. Even then, the berries won't be ready to pick until mid-June. Call the Scrivners at (573) 657-2989 to set up an appointment.

Make Your Own Fresh Blueberry Wine
By E. Crystal Cornell

❖

The following information was provided by the Scrivners to show you how to make blueberry wine. There are several resources that you'll need. Time and patience are the most important ones, since wine-making is a slow process. In addition, you'll need to buy certain equipment and supplies. It also helps to set aside a cool wine storage area. This space would also be handy for keeping the large fermenter bucket, which can take up space in your house.

Blueberry Wine, Recipe and Procedures
(makes five gallons)

Suggested equipment and supplies:

Sugar scale hydrometer
Fermentation bag
Lever-type corking machine
Bottles and Corks
Two 6-gallon polyfermenters
Yeast energizer
Pectic enzyme
Acid blend
Campden tablets
Potassium sorbate
Montrachet wine yeast

1) Dissolve 10 pounds of sugar in one gallon of water.
2) Mix with 4 gallons of water in fermenter; dissolve sugar. Add 5 campden tablets. Draw one gallon of the solution to be saved and added in step 7.
3) Crush 12 pounds of blueberries and strain through fermenter bag into fermenter. Keep pulp in fermenter bag, tie and place in fermenter.
4) Add: 7 teaspoons acid blend
   2 teaspoons pectic enzyme
   2 teaspoons energizer
   Stir and cover, but do not seal.
5) After 24 hours, add one package of Montrachet wine yeast.
6) Stir daily, squeeze fermenter bag and check specific gravity.
7) When specific gravity lowers to 1.03 (in about one week), squeeze fermenter bag and remove bag from fermenter. Transfer the wine to a clean fermenter; add the 1 gallon of sugar solution saved in step 2; dissolve and add 5 campden tablets; seal and add the air lock.
8) When fermentation is complete (in about four weeks, very little carbon dioxide bubbling through air lock), transfer to clean fermenter, measure specific gravity (should be approximately 1.000), taste for desired sweetness and adjust specific gravity (2 ounces sugar per gallon will raise specific gravity about .005 units).
   A final specific gravity of 1.000 to 1.002 will result in a dry wine. After adjustment, add 5 campden tablets, seal and reattach air lock.
9) After two or three months, transfer wine to a clean container, make a final adjustment of specific gravity, add potassium sorbate to prevent any further fermentation, and bottle.
   Supplies available from E. C. Kraus in Independence, Mo., at (816) 254-7448.

Hartsburg

Bikes • Food • Lodging • Parking • Phone • Post Office • Restrooms
Milepost 153
3.8 miles from Wilton to Hartsburg • 3.8 miles from Hartsburg to Claysville
Call Hartsburg Hitching Post for trail information: (573) 657-2847
Post Office: (573) 657-2300 • Zip Code: 65039

From the Highway: Take I-70 to Highway 63 south (at Columbia) to Route A, which is halfway to Jefferson City, and 3 miles past Ashland. On Route A, turn right and head 5 miles to Hartsburg.

Eats

Dotty's Café • Wheelchair accessible • Open Mon. - Fri. 9 a.m. - 8 p.m., Closed Tues. Sat. 7:30 a.m. - 8 p.m., Sun. 7:30 a.m. - 2 p.m. • (573) 657-4502

Hartsburg Hitching Post • 10 North Second • (573) 657-2847
Run by Jim and Patty Motter, the Hartsburg Hitching Post holds open bluegrass and country music jam sessions beginning at 2 p.m. every Sunday afternoon. Bring your instruments to pick and sing along, enjoy the beer, or just bring your ears to listen and your hands to clap in time.

Bicycle Rental

Hartsburg Bicycle Company
half a block north of the trailhead, on the east side of Second
P.O. Box 116 • (573) 657-4529 • To open Spring 1997

Bed & Breakfast

Globe Bed & Breakfast • between Dotty's Café and the trail
P.O. Box 89 • (573) 657-4529

Plenty o' pumpkins: There are pumpkins of all sizes for all sizes of people at Hartsburg's Pumpkin Fest each October. Here, Robert Adkins of Hallsville hands a pumpkin to his son, Bo, 5, as Trina Adkins, 3, watches.

Russell Sapp tills a field in Hartsburg that is traditionally used to grow pumpkins for the Pumpkin Festival in October. Last season's festival drew 20,000 people.

Surging Community
Hartsburg rebuilds after the flood

❖

Silence can be a powerful force. In '93, Hartsburg residents worked for months to fend off the raging Missouri River to preserve their town's most precious commodities — peace and quiet.

Unlike some devastated river towns, today Hartsburg is alive, well and re-building. Very few of the residents ever left. Most decided to stay.

A 100-year-old hotel has reopened its doors. A new post office was constructed. Homes have been rebuilt, new paint applied, and residents are close to getting back to life as it was before.

The bottom lands outside of town, however, were irrevocably changed. The levee road that followed the river is now a roller coaster turned on its side, zigging and zagging upon freshly constructed levees. Much of the bottom land has been replanted, but many sand dunes remain. The blowing sand has permeated everything in its wake. It is the only sound, as infinite particles tumble along to create a whisper like rain. It stands 10 feet deep in some places, unfarmable for years to come.

Where wheat once grew, huge bowls were cut into the rich topsoil by the river's restless wanderings. Lakes remain, great for fishing perhaps, but to farmers they're unwelcome additions that cost thousands of dollars in yearly crop losses.

Nevertheless, farming here has continued. New crops have been introduced to utilize the sandy soils. Sunflowers, with their long tap roots, have proven ideally suited for production here.

Though agriculture has long been Hartsburg's economic mainstay, the current population of 100 is but a shadow of the town's bustling past. It was in the late

1800s that German immigrants settled here in the fertile soil of the Missouri River bottoms. With the demise of river and train travel, the rhythm of the town has slowed dramatically. Before the advent of the car, the town had hosted two banks, a newspaper, and all the other amenities of a self-sustaining town. As people travelled more, area businesses couldn't compete with those in Columbia and Jefferson City.

The MFA gas station, which sold its last gallon of gas in 1968, stands as a testament to this forgotten boom. A rusted pump out front still displays the price of $6.10 through fogged glass.

Though the landscape of Hartsburg has fluctuated over the years, the people have remained a constant. Fritz Arnsmeyer has lived in Hartsburg most of his 82 years. He resides in the house his parents bought in 1919. Despite being flooded, he has no intention of leaving.

"Where was I going to go? When you live somewhere all your life it's hard to pick it up and leave," Arnsmeyer said. "There's mostly second and third generations left. You have to give 'em a lot of credit for staying.

"I've been through some floods before, but this was the first time we had water in the house," he said. "The flood of '51 lacked four to five feet to get to the house. This year we had three feet inside."

The river stayed long enough to ruin everything within reach. "A year or two will go by and Hartsburg will come back some. Not exactly like it was, but it'll come back," Arnsmeyer said.

The Globe Hotel, established in 1893, has reopened its doors to trail users. "I never had any doubt I would rebuild," said Jeanette Crawford, the owner. "It was half-restored and open before the flood and will be again. We held together during the flood because we had lots of support from everyone."

The 16-room hotel was under six feet of water. "There were tons of mud inside. It was like chocolate pudding. It stuck to everything and wouldn't move out," she said.

Hartsburg

Hartsburg's revitalization has also been aided by volunteers nationwide. The United Church of Christ has sent four groups of students to the town to work during their spring breaks.

One week, 40 students and seven adults from New Hampshire picked up debris and dug out a buried center-pivot irrigating system.

"Missouri made sense because of the flood," said Adam Duclos, a New Hampshire student. "We did the menial jobs, so they could get to important things like fixing levees."

These students were but the last in a wave of thousands of volunteers who inundated the flooded town to help out.

Jim Sauro, a plumber from Vineland, N.J., and 10 other volunteer plumbers from his state spent a week in Hartsburg last year overhauling bathrooms and kitchens. "Imagine how easy it could have been to give up," Sauro said. "These are strong people and we've gained strength from them. You can't buy this feeling," he said. "It has definitely changed our lives a thousand times over."

Hartsburg Baptist Church, built in 1900, had eight feet of water in the sanctuary and four feet of water in the education wing.

The flood damage was more severe at Peace United Church of Christ. The basement had 12 feet of water in it, and the sanctuary contained two feet of water. Damage to the church was estimated at $100,000, said Bryan Crousore, the pastor. He also discovered some exotic fauna.

"In our basement of mud, we had lots of unsavory creatures swimming around like frogs and snakes," Crousore said.

Members of the two churches were forced out of their buildings. During that time, Hartsburg Baptist Church held services both inside and outside of the Hartsburg Fire Station, and Peace United Church of Christ held services at the Optimists Club in Ashland.

While things are almost back to normal at Hartsburg Baptist and Peace United, members of both churches said they will not forget how many people helped out after the flood. "The church looks at least as good if not better than it did last year," said Crousore.

"People came from Pennsylvania to New Mexico." Crousore said. "We couldn't have done it without the volunteers."

The Hartsburg Hitching Post was saved by volunteers. Sandbaggers built a wall as high as 10 feet between the river and the business. Owners Jim and Patty Motter kept it open 24 hours a day during the effort to make coffee, sell beer, and let volunteers use the bathroom.

"There were lots of tears, lots of confusion and lots of encouragement," Patty Motter said. "The mood was manic. Working for 14 hours, sleeping for two, up for 14 more.

"We had this type of support group getting together three times per day," she said. "I bet that's why we held together. When someone got discouraged we were there for them. It's a real special town. We were held together by the whole experience."

Martha Hesse moved to Hartsburg from Germany 60 years ago. Though this was the worst flood she's seen, she wanted to stay here. "This is where I have been for most of my life," she said.

Tom Mericle's house was almost completely covered by the flood waters. Instead of moving, he lifted his house more than seven feet and then began the arduous task of renovating it.

"What set us apart from some others were the organizations and the people we had helping us out," said farmer Terry Hilgedick. "The firehouse was serving three meals a day for five months, and food was coming in from every direction. We didn't even have to ask."

The flood gutted his home in the bottoms. A forgotten book entitled "How to Plan Your Financial Future" lies upon the mud-caked floor of his old home. Renovating both his parents' house and his new home in town has taken up most of his spare time. Volunteers have also helped the Hilgedicks cope with the flood.

"The Salvation Amy did a ton down here. For six straight months they had two people working in Hartsburg full time," he said.

One man from Pennsylvania came five times and brought a total of 20 people with him, Hilgedick said. People from Versailles came every Saturday for a couple of months to help with the clean-up, as well.

After seeing everyone pull together, "I'd lean more towards going someplace and helping out than I would have before," Hilgedick said.

Blue Jay

True to her
Rural Routes...

By Jennifer Plunkett of the *Columbia Missourian*

❖

As a letter carrier for the Hartsburg post office,
Linda Nahler delivers to 471 mailboxes on 83 miles
of gravel roads along the Missouri River.

Having grown up with the folks to whom she delivers, letter carrier Linda Nahler is true to her rural routes.

Straddled across the middle of her white, F-150 Ford truck, Linda Nahler drives one-legged and one-handed. She uses her left hand to manipulate the steering wheel and her left foot to control the pedals. Nahler's right leg holds bulky packages in place on the truck's floor. Her right arm is moving constantly — in and out of the passenger's side window.

Nahler drives around like this by choice. "That's the life of a rural mail carrier," says Nahler, who lives in Ashland.

Nahler is a post office on wheels. Every day, she's enveloped by an average of 2,000 bills, letters, coupons, magazines and catalogs. By 3 p.m. that deluge of mail will be delivered to 471 mailboxes throughout Hartsburg and Wilton.

Nahler doesn't like to make her customers wait. "The customers are the most important part of my job. So I try to stay on schedule as best I can."

And she does. Hartsburg Postmaster Dan Williams says Nahler is the fastest, most efficient rural mail carrier he has ever seen.

The speedy deliverer starts to case, or sort her mail, at 7:30 a.m.

"I grew up around here, and I think that's what made it easier for me to learn the route when I started," she says. "A lot of the people on the route are people I went to school with or people I just knew already, so it makes it easier to remember where they live."

By 9:20 a.m. she's found a temporary home in her truck for 2,000 pieces of mail. Then it's time to hit the road.

Winding her way through the twisting roads of her route, Nahler finds herself surrounded by bundles and bundles of sorted mail and being greeted by friends — of the animal sort.

"A lot of days, I see wildlife — turkeys, deer," she says. Nahler is even greeted by slithering snakes, corpulent cows and gawking guinea fowl. One time it was a little critter that stopped her from doing her job. Nahler was bitten by a black spider, and her right hand swelled up, forcing her to call in sick for work.

"The trees are getting real pretty now," she says. "That's one of the advantages of being a rural carrier. You get to see the spring budding and flowers and autumn leaves and the colors."

"I'm a farm girl, you see, so most of my growing up was outside," she says. "In summertime, we were always in the hay fields. And I've never really left the outdoors."

Three-quarters of her route is made up of gravel. Trading in her truck for a new one every two years is a normal part of her job.

"There are many rainy days when I've found myself fixing a flat. One day, I even got two flats."

For situations like that, Nahler keeps two tires with her at all times. And two tanks of gas. Nahler covers more than 80 miles of puddle-patched, mud-caked and ice-laden roads on her route, with her window open.

"The winter driving is the most difficult aspect of the job. The snow I can handle. I don't like the ice very well."

No accidents so far. Knock on a mailbox.

For five hours a day, five days a week, Nahler is driving alone in her truck — with a 15-minute break and without a complaint.

"Sometimes there are honeybees, ducks or chicks to deliver," she said. "Once, I even had a car fender."

Nahler's mother and father live two miles east of Hartsburg in Slate Creek, the place of her birth. She delivers mail to her parents every day. "It's just real neat to be able to see them all the time," Nahler says. She even stops for a quick lunch.

"She won't sit down at the table for lunch, no way," says her mother, Gladys Martin. "She'll take a piece of pie or cornbread that I've made and eat it and go right on."

Nahler's customers stop to say hi to her, too. "She's like home-folk around here to me," Hazel Holton of Wilton says. "Linda's just a nice, sweet person, and she does a good job. I really like talking to her."

Nahler's day isn't done when she completes her route. Nahler and her family farm corn, milo, wheat and soybeans on more than 1,000 acres.

Nahler says she's pleased with the hours of effort she puts in and pounds of work she does every day. The payoff is tremendous at work and in her heart.

"People appreciate what you do and show it," she says. "They'll put a plate of cookies or candy out for me, and that's always nice. That means more to me than anything."

From the *Columbia Missourian*, November 11, 1994

It's a Big One!
By Chris Carroll

❖

The first thing you think when you see a 102-pound monster watermelon isn't how good a cool, juicy slice would taste on a hot August day. Your first thought is that you wouldn't want the thing to roll off the table onto your foot.

Russell Sapp, who grows produce when not working at his job of driving a dumptruck, is proud of the 102-pounder, but you wouldn't call him ecstatic. He expects more and bigger things this year from his 30-by-60-foot watermelon patch in Hartsburg.

"There's another one out in them weeds that I think is maybe going to beat this one," Sapp says, pointing toward a green and yellow hulk protruding from the leaves.

Over the years, Sapp has grown three melons that weighed 105 pounds each. "I was hoping this one would beat my old record. These are a new type I'm growing — called Carolina Cross — and they're supposed to get up to 200 pounds. I'd like to beat that and show the seed company they were wrong," Sapp said. "And I'm planning on putting in 2 or 3 acres of these next year."

Sapp and his son, Keith, have been growing watermelons on and off for 20 years. They have 10 acres of normal-sized watermelons planted in the bottom land of the Missouri River. But it's the big ones that hold a special place in their hearts.

"I once took three watermelons to the Boone County Fair, and I took first, second and third place. There were a lot of people wanted to enter that contest, but when they took one look at the size of mine, they just left."

The main buyers of the mighty melons will be owners of roadside stands, said Keith Sapp. They'll use them to draw in crowds.

"You know, I could sell 100 of them tomorrow if I had 100," he said. "But you don't make a profit because you can't grow enough of them on the plant. Besides, they're awfully hard to move."

So how do they taste?

"We're gonna have a party with it, or try to, if it's any good." Russell Sapp said. "If it ain't, we'll just cut some smaller ones and eat them instead."

From the *Columbia Missourian,* August 18, 1994

Pickin' Pun'kins

Hartsburg's annual Pumpkin Festival has turned this small town into Missouri's favorite pumpkin pickin' place.

Hartsburg began growing pumpkins in 1912, when August Klemme planted half an acre to feed his hogs. Today, Hartsburg has two major pumpkin growers, the Russell Sapp and Norlan Hackman families. The fertile, sandy soil here produces large pumpkin harvests.

Pumpkins are planted in mid-June and normally ripen in mid-to-late September. Nearly 100,000 pumpkins were grown and harvested in 1996. After harvest, tractor trailers haul many of the pumpkins off to cities. Others go to local stores to be sold as jack-o'-lanterns. Types of pumpkins grown in Hartsburg include Connecticut, Field, Howden, Baby Pam Pie, Jack Be Little and Big Max.

Come join other pumpkin hunters and venture out to see fall's rainbow and Hartsburg's harvest in 1997. Between 30,000 and 50,000 people turned out for the two-day event in 1996. (Be warned: if you come by car, leave plenty of time for the traffic jam. In 1996, it started all the way out at Highway 63. Or come the back route, along the river road through Wilton.)

During the festival, jack-o'-lantern hunters milled around thousands of plump pumpkins lining the streets. The Pumpkin Committee organized a parade and apple-butter cooking contest. Pumpkins were on sale for carving, eating and picking in patches throughout the town. The town was filled with booths selling apple butter, hot dogs and funnel cakes. And there were, of course, pumpkin pies, pumpkin breads, pumpkin cookies and cakes.

Claysville

No services
3.8 miles from Hartsburg to Claysville
6.6 miles from Claysville to North Jefferson

A few miles past Hartsburg you will pass Claysville. There are no services here for the trail user, but it still deserves mention.

When the river port shipping town of Stonesport was washed away in 1844, the residents moved further back from the river. This new town was named Claysville. Its economy was fueled by burgeoning river travel and trade. When the MK&T railroad came through in 1892, Hartsburg was established as a rail shipping center. Businesses in Claysville migrated to Hartsburg. Only a few structures now remain.

There is more to life than speeding it up.
— *Gandhi*

Cedar City
(a.k.a. North Jefferson)
Food • Parking • Picnic Table • Restrooms • Water
Milepost 143
6.6 miles from Claysville to Cedar City • 6 miles from Cedar City to Wainwright
Post Office: (573) 635-9764 • Zip Code: 65022
From the Highway: Take I-70 to Highway 63 south.

Eats
MFA Agri Services • Look for the grain bins • 1009 Fourth Street (573) 635-7183
Snacks, phone and restroom • Mon.-Fri. 8 a.m. - 5 p.m., Sat. 8 a.m. - 12 p.m.

Cedar City was all but washed away by the flood of 1993. In fact, its name seems to have already been relegated to history, as most people from the area now refer to it as North Jefferson because it was incorporated in 1989 by Jefferson City. The MK&T Railroad also referred to it as North Jefferson.

Cedar City was laid out in 1866 by David Kinney, owner of the Cedar City Land Company. As early as 1825 there was a post office located here, which was called Hibernia. (What?!?) In 1870 the town became incorporated, and in 1872 it changed its name to Cedar City.

The Chicago and Alton Railroad line running from Mexico, Missouri, arrived in Cedar City in 1872 and terminated here. Cedar City soon had two railroad depots. Passengers unloaded from the train here, and a horse trolley took them to the ferry to cross the river to Jefferson City. In the 1890s, a toll bridge was built.

The Katy Trail doesn't actually go through North Jefferson proper. The town is located one mile south of the trail. It is accessible by the newly constructed Jefferson City Greenway, which is a one-mile extension of the Katy Trail up to the road in North Jefferson.

Along this new greenway expansion, there is a brand-new picnic shelter replete with picnic tables, restrooms, drinking fountain and spigot. From there, Jefferson City proper is still across the river but not completely out of reach. Before crossing the bridge, read the **Jefferson City** section.

See **Bikers Bulletin Board** for services on this side of the bridge.

A farmer works the earth under the watchful eye of Ceres, the Greek goddess of grain and agriculture, who adorns the Capitol's dome.

Jefferson City

Bikes • Food • Gas • Lodging • Parking • Post Office • Restrooms • Shuttle Service
Off the trail (other side of river, no walkway on bridge)
South on Highway 54 approx. 2 miles
Trail Information: 1 (800) 334-6946
Post Office: (573) 681-9292 • Zip Codes: 65101, 65102, 65109

Directions: Take I-70 to Highway 63 south. Or I-70 to Highway 54 south.

Bed & Breakfast

Jefferson Inn B&B
801 West High Street
1 (800) 530-5009 or (573) 635-7196
HOT TUB!
Rates: $60-125.

Shuttle Service

Trailblazers Bike Rentals & Pick-Up and Delivery
(573) 659-2749
Be prepared to leave a message and for Vail Kinsaul to call you back. This works best when calling in advance several days before you need a lift.

Services

Services and lodging here are similar to those found in any large city and are far too numerous to list. For specific hotel and service information, call the Chamber of Commerce and Visitors Bureau at (573) 634-3616, or the Missouri Division of Tourism at (573) 751-4133. See **Bikers Bulletin Board** for more information.

The Thomas Hart Benton murals entitled "A Social History
of the State of Missouri" are located in the Capitol building.

Jefferson City

There is no walkway on the Missouri River bridge at Jefferson City. The silver bridge does have a very wide shoulder, however, and several local riders use this to cross the river. This approach is definitely not recommended for families or heart patients. If you decide to cross the bridge, *walk* your bike across. I've done it and it's not bad at all, even in heavy traffic.

If you decide to ride across, cross the river on the silver bridge, ride up the first "entrance" ramp and you will be just minutes from the Capitol building. If you continue forward off the entrance ramp, you will be on Clay Street, which drops you at the doorstep of the Jefferson Inn B&B two blocks later.

If you're looking for a little shelter from the storm at the trip's half-way point, I can't think of a better place to settle your bones, order pizza and swap war stories while soaking in the hot tub. Innkeeper Ruth Schaefer makes you feel at home.

Some visitors to our online site said several hotels across the river in Jefferson City are happy to pick up bike riders and shuttle them to their hotel for the night. There is a phone available at the MFA in Cedar City during work hours (see **Cedar City** listing or look for the grain silos). These hotels include but are not limited to the following: Capitol Plaza Hotel 1 (800) 338-8088; the Ramada Inn 1 (800) 392-0202; and the Jefferson Inn B&B 1 (800) 530-5009. You may even be able to get a lift for a minimal charge if you are not staying at their hotel. Otherwise, try calling Trailblazers on the previous above.

Note: With Trailblazers and the Jefferson Inn B&B, make arrangements beforehand, since there are times when no one is attending the phone during the day.

Upon visiting Jefferson City, you can say you've been to the only state capital that isn't located on an interstate. "Jeff" City also holds the distinction of having more letters than any other state's capital. (I learned this from a North Carolinian.)

During the era of river trade, Missouri's first state Capitol was located in St. Charles, near the confluence of the Missouri and the Mississippi Rivers. As the state's

population stretched ever farther westward, the Capitol was moved to a more centralized location, in the heart of the Show Me State. See the **St. Charles** section for more history of our capital.

The current Capitol was built in MCMXIII (1913 for those of us who never learned to read Roman numerals). In 1911, lightning struck the dome of the previous Capitol, started a fire and leveled it. The current Capitol is modeled after its bigger counterpart in D.C. (which does lie near the interstate, so I've been told).

The Capitol building is perhaps the only government building to be constructed *under* budget. Remaining funds were used to commission artists to decorate the structure. The interior is an amazing pictoral of Missouri's past, brought to life through the work of Frank Brangwyn, N. C. Wyeth, James Earle Fraser, Alexander Stirling Calder and the famous work by Thomas Hart Benton painted in 1936.

The Capitol also houses a free, self-guided State Museum, (573) 751-4127. A half-hour led tour on weekdays includes seeing the Thomas Hart Benton murals. The Capitol also sells books covering all aspects of Missouri life and history.

The Governor's Mansion is within walking distance from the Capitol. This was built to mirror the architectural mastery of Rivercene, located in Boonville, also near the Katy. If time permits, have a look on Tuesdays and Thursdays from 10 a.m. to noon and 1 to 3 p.m. Tours are free but call ahead (573) 751-7929.

Upon heading east from Jefferson City, you will be leaving the Manitou Bluffs region and heading into Missouri's Rhineland country. This region extends through the most well-preserved German towns along the Missouri River and takes you by some of Missouri's famous vineyards and wineries.

Campers' Note: Binder Lake, (573) 634-6482, off Highway 50 west, is 2 miles past Capitol Mall. There are 18 full-hookups, showers and laundry. Mariosa Delta Campground, (573) 455-2452, is 10 miles east of Jeff, on Highway 50. Their services are similar. The Jaycee Fairgrounds, (573) 893-3950, two miles south of Highway 50 West, on Fairgrounds Road, is open to large group camping.

Wainwright

No services

6 miles from Cedar City to Wainwright • 6 miles from Wainwright to Tebbetts

From the Highway: From I-70 take Highway 54 to Route 94 east.

Wainwright's main street dead-ends 100 yards into town and promptly turns into a private drive. There doesn't appear to be much here for the average trail user, although the small white church is worth a look. Platted in 1892 as a railroad town, Wainwright was originally called Linkville. During railroad construction, its name was changed to Wainwright after Ellis Wainwright, a St. Louis capitalist. Heading east, the bluffs diminish here a bit, giving way to more pastoral surrounds.

If you are looking for a fun diversion, I'd recommend following the "honey for sale" signs. In addition to signs, you may see stacks of white boxes on private properties, where the honey is cultivated. For every pound of honey that bees produce, they must collect pollen from 2 million flowers. (Hence the saying Busy as Bees?)

The many bee hives along this stretch of the trail recall earlier days when bees were important to the economy. The honeybee well known in Missouri was originally brought from Europe. Native Americans called them "the white man's fly." Hunting for bees that had escaped their keepers and colonized in the wild was a source of livelihood in pioneer days. Early writers described bee trees that yielded 50 gallons of honey apiece. Honey and beeswax were principal exports for some settlements. Bees were so important to local Missouri economies, in fact, that in another part of the state, an Iowa-Missouri border war, The Honey War, was supposedly ignited when a Missourian cut down bee trees claimed by both states.

After passing Wainwright, the next good stop comes a mile and a half down the road. A quick veer up the gravel road to the left at the Bakersville Christian Church sign will lead you 500 yards up to a pristine rest spot near a nice church.

The old outhouse (not for use) has the best view any outhouse possibly could. This is a good place to have lunch, take a break or take a nap. This is also the best place to view the hill known as Cote Sans Dessein.

Cote Sans Dessein

About two miles after crossing the Rivaux Creek bridge, keep an eye out for a geologic anomaly south across the flood plain. Called *Cote sans Dessein* (hill without design) by early Missouri French, this large hill protrudes from the middle of the flood plain. This is the only point to survive the scourge of the meandering Missouri River within the entire River Valley.

Though today it appears as only a green island, a small group of Frenchmen settled here about three years before H. M. Breckenridge and Manuel Lisa passed through this region in 1811. They penned the following description:

"The Cote Sans Dessein is a beautiful place situated on the N.E. side of the river and in sight of the Osage (River). The name is given to the place from the circumstance of a single detached hill filled with limestone and standing on the bank of the river about 600 yards long and very narrow. The village has been established about 3 years. There are 13 French families and two or three Indians. They have handsome fields in the prairies, but the greater part of their time is spent hunting."

When Missouri considered moving its Capitol, Cote Sans Dessein was considered a fitting place. But it's chances for state politics were soon dashed by greedy land speculators — some holding office — who had bought up the land, hoping to cash in on the new site. Numerous individuals claimed title to the same land, which eased the decision to place Missouri's Capitol across the river in Jefferson City.

Interestingly enough, another town along the Katy Trail was also considered as a possible site for the Capitol. Do you know which one? (Answer: Rocheport)

Rivaux Creek

Rivaux Creek between Wainwright and Tebbetts

Tebbetts

Bike Repair • Food • Gas • Parking • Picnic Table • Post Office
Milepost 131
6 miles from Wainwright to Tebbetts • 6.2 miles from Tebbetts to Mokane
Turner's Store for trail information: (573) 295-6112
Post Office: (573) 295-4866 • Zip Code: 65080
Directions: From I-70, take Highway 54 south to BB south to Route 94 east.

Eats

The Turner's Store
Past grain elevators, next to the post office
(573) 295-6112
Mon.-Sat. 7 a.m. - 6 p.m., Sun. 8 a.m. - noon

Tebbetts was platted as a railroad town in 1892. The town was named Tebbetts after an officer of the construction company that built the railroad. The depot (demolished in 1963) was completed in 1893 and the first train arrived in June of that year. By 1894, Tebbetts had a post office. Like so many other towns along the trail, its heyday was vibrant but short-lived. Commercial interests were attracted to larger towns. All that remains today is an outpost of the past.

Large grain elevators signal your arrival in Tebbetts. Several covered picnic tables are nearby along Highway 94.

Mrs. Turner opened her store in 1933. She stays busy
running it, making sandwiches and selling antiques.

Turn your watch back
half a century at Turner's Store

❖

The store is spotless. Not a speck of dirt or dust touches the canned goods.
There's two of everything, all neatly in rows. The Turner's Store in Tebbetts,
population 200 "or so," is a great place to visit.

At age 91, Mrs. Turner still runs the store, the register and serves up fresh deli
sandwiches. "I've never talked about retiring," she said.

"Now, I don't *cook*, but I do serve a world of sandwiches here," she said.
"I've got potato salad, cakes and cookies, you name it."

Two brooms lean against the "Bank of Tebbetts Bank Vault" in the back
corner, reminding you that you are in Tebbett's old bank building. The bank opened
its door in 1906 but folded in 1929 with the advent of the stock market crash and
Great Depression.

"My husband and I opened this store in '33," she said. "There were 3 stores
here then. Tebbetts sold ice, had a barber shop and a lodge hall. We even had a
Ford dealership."

"We made our own electricity back then — Mr. Turner was pretty talented
about things like that."

So you had the first electric lights in Tebbetts?

"Oh yes."

"We bought that ice case new in 1939," she said, pointing to the meats and cheeses. "Now everybody wants everything packaged, but it makes the meat taste bad."

Tebbetts is the only town between St. Charles and Kansas City that never floods. "The lay of the land keeps the water from creeping up," she said.

However, the surrounding farmlands are not as fortunate.

"Then the floods began in the 40s — not like in 1903, but it began to flood every few years, so people started moving off their farms. Their children go in to town to work and marry and go off, so it's not growing so fast."

About every other customer is a stranger, Mrs. Turner said. "We get so many people coming through visiting. A couple from Oregon came in yesterday and went on and on about how they had never seen a country store like this. 'Course I don't keep it like I should, but I sure try."

As for business off the trail: "I can't handle what I have. Somedays I sell 30 sandwiches at noon. That's enough."

"When that trail is finally opened [from end to end], I hope they [opponents of the Katy Trail] change. Tebbetts could sure grow if people want it to. I hope it amounts to a little somethin'."

On another note, Mrs. Turner has donated the building next door to the YMCA. This two-story building is 21 by 51 feet. It was a general store and a church. Anyone interested in using this building or donating to the restoration, contact Charley Davidson at the Conservation Federation at (573) 634-2322. Or, David Steinmeyer at the Jefferson City YMCA at (573) 761-9009.

Campers' Note: Mrs. Turner says she *sometimes* allows considerate and respectful trail-users to pitch a tent on her adjacent property, when they ask first.

Tebbetts' "Main Street"

Mokane

Food • Gas • Parking • Post Office • Restrooms
Milepost 125
6.2 miles from Tebbetts to Mokane • 5 miles from Mokane to Steedman
Post Office: (573) 676-5881 • Zip Code: 65059
From the Highway: Take I-70 to Highway 63 south to Route 94 east
or I-70 to Highway 54 south to Route C.

Eats

K.D. Trail Grill • on left side of road coming into town • (573) 676-3073

Originally known as St. Auberts and Smith Landing, this settlement dates back to 1818, when the town was located closer to the river. With the advent of the railroad, the town held a contest on June 6, 1893, to rename the town. A prize was awarded for the winning name of MissOuri, KANsas and Eastern, which soon became part of the MK&T Railroad. Shortly thereafter, Mokane became an overnight boomtown. The town soon had a school, two churches, a bank, a drugstore, three physicians and two blacksmith shops. In 1894, a newspaper was established called the *Herald Post,* which later became the *Mokane Missourian.* In 1908, MK&T made Mokane a division headquarters.

Mokane's prosperity lasted well into the 1920s. The population had grown to over a thousand people and the town was well on its way towards rivalling the nearby cities of Fulton and Mexico. However, the changes of transit technology crushed the town's boom just as quickly as it had begun. In the 1920s, MK&T decided to move its division headquarters farther west to Sedalia. This loss, coupled with the onset of the Great Depression, left Mokane to revert to a small center of trade. Mokane is now essentially a residential hub serving Fulton and Jefferson City, with a current population of 186.

Bikers' Note: Mokane has covered picnic tables right off the trail. Behind K.D. Trail's restaurant, there is a coin-operated car wash (with sprayers) called Huck's Car Wash. The Missouri River fishing access for Mokane is approximately

one mile before town and is a good road for getting down within sight of the river. There's a sort of barge graveyard there too, to check out if you're so inclined.

Mel Wilson takes aim during Steedman's bimonthly Meat Shoot, where competitors shoot paper targets using different game shot. On competition day, there's usually huge barbecue grills brought in, so stop in and check it out.

Steedman

Food • Parking • Post Office
5 miles from Mokane to Steedman • 7 miles from Steedman to Portland
Call S.O.B.'s Bar & Grill for trail information: (573) 676-3220
Post Office: (573) 676-5717 • Zip Code: 65077
From the Highway: From I-70, take Highway 54 south
to Route O to Route CC south.

Eats

S.O.B.'s Bar & Grill • directly across from trail • (573) 676-3220

Steedman was platted in 1892 as a railroad town, and was named to honor Dr. I. G. W. Steedman. The St. Louisan owned several thousand acres in the area west of Portland.

It had a post office in 1894, a bank in 1915 and several stores. Today Steedman consists of a few dozen residences and a restaurant lovingly referred to as S.O.B.'s Bar, short for Steedman's Only Bar. They have a full menu and a pool table. The barbecue sandwiches here can't be beat.

Campers' Note: Sometimes people camp in the grassy area in front of S.O.B.'s. Ask for permission at the bar. No bathroom.

Portland

Camping • Food • Parking • Post Office • Restrooms
7 miles from Steedman to Portland • 2 miles from Portland to Bluffton
Post Office: (573) 676-5831 • Zip Code: 65067
From the Highway: Take I-70 to Route D (near Williamsburg) south.

Eats

Riverfront Bar & Grill
Mon.-Sat. 8 a.m. - 9 p.m., Sun. noon - 8 p.m.
(573) 676-3271

Campground

Opening scheduled for 1997
See **Campers' Note** next page for details.
(573) 676-5396.

Portland was a thriving river town, established in 1831. Portland was the only town of importance in Callaway County along the river before the railroad came, but once the route was established, the railroad towns of Wainwright, Tebbetts, Mokane and Steedman quickly appeared.

Count Adelbert Baudissin, thinking it was an up-and-coming town in the Missouri River Valley, settled near Portland in the 1850s. In an account he states, "the thing for me to do is to direct German emigrants to Portland because I have the firm conviction that business people as well as landowners would find their good fortune at this place." At the time the population of Portland was around 200, and eight to ten riverboats docked at the town each week. The town continued to thrive when the railroad came through. According to a local resident, the town's depot was quite nice with a large waiting room. But it was later torn down, and replaced by a "little two by four thing."

Campers' Note: A lot of people camp at the riverfront. Follow the river access road to get there. Resident Steve Hunt is also planning to operate a campground in Portland beginning Spring 1997. This campground is 2 blocks north of the trail by the Episcopalian church. He is planning to have showers, bathrooms, bike rental and sales. He also plans to have group camping areas and picnic tables. He also mentioned interest in helping bikers with shuttles on a part-time basis. Before setting arrival dates and hard-to-meet expectations, call Steve for the complete low down to confirm what services are available: (573) 676-5396.

Bluffton

• Lodging •
Milepost 111
2 miles from Portland to Bluffton • 11 miles from Bluffton to McKittrick

Bed & Breakfast
Rendleman Home B&B • Rt. 1 Box 27, Rhineland, MO 65069 • (573) 236-4575

Bluffton is off to the north of the trail. Your greeting party may only consist of a stray dog or two, since the town itself contains just a few houses. The huge 100-foot-high bluffs here make for some spectacular scenery for the next four miles. This stretch was opened in September 1996.

Campers' Note: The Rendlemans' B&B has camping spaces available for up to 10 people. They've put in two bathrooms in their barn, behind their B&B, and hope to have a kitchen completed by summer. Call ahead for more information.

Many of the original railroad trusses are still in place. Look for a plaque showing what year the trusses were constructed. Many were built in the 1920s and earlier.

Rhineland

Food • Parking • Post Office
Post Office: (573) 236-4330 • Zip Code: 65069
From the Highway: Take I-70 south to Highway 19 then west on Route 94.

Eats
Gosen Store • Located right on the trail • (573) 236-4411

R hineland is pretty much gone. New Rhineland is being born. The flood decimated this town with 63 inches of water. Up the hill, you'll see the site where 10 of the surviving structures are being moved. This area will be called New Rhineland, where much of the town will be relocated. As for the five-block stretch of devastated homes, it will be bulldozed under and reverted to farmland. Once the town is relocated, there are plans to develop a trailside campground, sometime in the near future.

The Meyers Hilltop Farm B&B is located in McKittrick.

McKittrick
No services • Milepost 100 • Zip Code: 65056
11 miles from Bluffton to McKittrick • 16.4 miles from McKittrick to Treloar

T he town of McKittrick is located across the Missouri River from Hermann and appears to have been an early settlement. Other than the B&B above, there are no services here for trail users.

During the summer months, the rolling hills of Hermann play host to visitors enjoying the area's festivities and wineries.

Hermann

Bikes • Crafts • Camping • Food • Gas • Lodging • Parking
Post Office • Restrooms • RV Park • Wineries
Off the trail (other side of river, no walkway on bridge)
Hermann Tourism Visitor's Center: 1 (800) 932-8687
Post Office: (573) 486-2798 • Zip Code: 65041
From the Highway: Take I-70, then south on Highway 19.

Eats
Everything from Burger Haus to Subway to fine dining.

Bed & Breakfasts
There are 40 B&Bs in Hermann (up from only three about a decade ago). Call the Visitor Information Center at (573) 486-2744 for more details.

Lodging
The Captain Wohlt Inn
123 East Third St.
(573) 486-3357

Die Gillig Helmat (Homestead)
15 miles south of Hermann on Highway W
HCR 62, Box 30
(573) 943-6942

W i n e r i e s

Adam Puchta Winery
Highway 100 West
(573) 486-2361

Hermannhoff Winery & Vineyards
330 East 1st Street
(573) 486-5959

Stone Hill Winery
Stone Hill Highway
southwest corner of town
Rt. 1 Box 26
(573) 486-2221

RV Park & Campground

Hermann City Park • (573) 486-5827 and 486-5400
Located at the junction of Highways 19/100 and Gasconade Street.
For RVs, there are 24 hookups with water and electric. Full hookups with sewer
are $13; just electric $10 per night.
For tents there's a plot for tents next to the bathhouse (hot and cold water and
showers). Barbecue pits. Tents $8 a night. Closed November through April 1.

Hermann was founded in 1836 by the German Settlement Society of Philadelphia, whose members were appalled at the loss of native customs and language among their countrymen in America. This "Second Fatherland" was intended to be a self-supporting refuge for German heritage and tradition.

The proposed community was set up as a joint-stock company and was advertised throughout the United States and Germany. The colony quickly attracted a variety of professionals, artisans and laborers, drawn by the idea of a "German Athens of the West."

On behalf of the society, one member acquired 11,300 acres of Frene Creek Valley land for $15,612. His choice for the site, bounded by hills and bluffs on three sides and the Missouri River on the north, and teeming with wild grapevines, was apparently influenced by its similarity to the Rhine River region in Germany.

Anxious to begin on what they expected to become one of the largest cities in the United States, the Society modeled the layout of the colony on that of Philadelphia. Selecting the name of Germany's national hero, Hermann (Arminius in Latin), who defeated the Roman legion in 9 A.D., seemed a fitting symbol for the great dream their new settlement embodied.

By the turn of the century, Hermann had the third-largest winery in the world (second in the United States), producing 1,250,000 gallons a year, and was winning international gold medals for its wine. Today, the German heritage of Hermann is as strong as ever. Almost every weekend during the summer months, Hermann plays host to some sort of German festival. The biggest ones are Maifest and Octoberfest. Call the Visitors Center for exact dates.

Intersection of Highways 19 and 94 (Hermann)

Bikers' Note: The only bridge crossing the Missouri River between Boonville and Washington occurs on Highway 19 at Hermann. Though Hermann is across the river, there are a few services located at the Junction of Highways 19 and 94, close to the Katy Trail. There is a Loutre Market Grocery store and car wash here, and the grocery store might be a good place to hitch a ride across the bridge into Hermann in the back of somebody's pickup.

I've successfully ridden my bike across the Highway 19 bridge, but I did it with a van "escort" driving behind me with their flashers on. If you decide to ride your bike across the bridge, which has no bike lane, I would only recommend doing so if you can get someone to drive behind you with their blinkers on. This was a highlight of my last trip!

Treloar

Bikes • Food • Lodging • Parking • Post Office • Restrooms
Milepost 85
16.4 miles from McKittrick to Treloar • 3 miles from Treloar to Peers
Call Scenic Cycles, in Marthasville, for trail information: (314) 433-2909
Post Office: (314) 932-4227 or 932-4611 • Zip Code: 63378
From the Highway: From I-70 take Route 47 south to Route N.

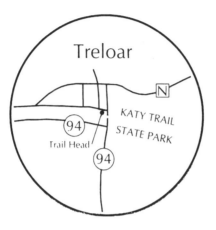

Eats

Our Place Restaurant & Bar • Right on the trail
P.O. Box 3 • (314) 932-4888
Mon.-Sat. 8 a.m. - 11 p.m., Sun. 11 a.m. - 8 p.m.

Bicycles

Blue House Bike Rentals • One block north of trail
(314) 932-4129 • 9 a.m. - 8 p.m. daily, weather permitting

Bed & Breakfast

Windhomme Hill B&B • Schomberg Road
1 (800) 633-0582 or (314) 932-4234 • HOT TUB!
Rates: $95-145.

Treloar was named after William Treloar, a former teacher at Hardin College in Mexico, Missouri, and the first Republican to be elected from the Ninth Congressional district. Our Place Restaurant has real good hamburgers, and specials on steaks Friday nights.

Peers

Food • Lodging • Parking • Restrooms
3 miles from Treloar to Peers • 4 miles from Peers to Marthasville
For trail information, call the Marthasville Chamber of Commerce
at (314) 433-5242 or Scenic Cycles at (314) 433-2909

Eats

Glosemeyer Store
19 Concord Hill Road
(314) 932-4655

Bed & Breakfasts

Concord Hill B&B
473 Concord Hill Road
(314) 932-4228 • HOT TUB!

The town of Peers was named after Judge Charles E. Peers, an attorney for the railroad and founder of the *Warrenton Banner* newspaper.

Wildflowers accompany trail riders throughout much of the spring season.

Marthasville is located right along the trail. The huge letters W-I-N-E-R-Y on the grain elevator are a distinctive touch. The rest area here has several picnic tables and downtown is only five feet away.

Marthasville

Bikes • Food • Gas • Lodging • Parking • Post Office • Restrooms
Shelter with Picnic Tables • Shuttle Service • Water • Winery
Milepost 78
4 miles from Peers to Marthasville • 3.7 miles from Marthasville to Dutzow
Call Marthasville Chamber of Commerce for trail information: (314) 433-5242
Post Office: (314) 433-2272 • Zip Code: 63357
From the Highway: From I-70, take Route 47 south.

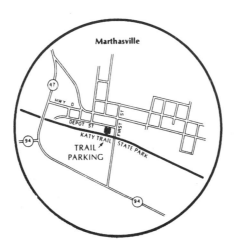

Marthasville

E a t s

Fudge Factory • Depot Street
Fudge, ice cream, baked goods and sugar-free pies

Loretta's Place • 201 Two Street
P.O. Box 162 • (314) 433-5775

Ole Town Inn
Depot Street

S & R Convenience
Highway 47
(314) 433-5443

Twin Gables
101 West Highway 47

B i c y c l e   R e n t a l   &   P o s s i b l e   S h u t t l e

Scenic Cycles • 203 Depot Street
(314) 433-2909 • Fax: 433-5131
Rental, sales, repair and driver/shuttle service with minimum 24-hour notice.
Will shuttle your car to end destination. Call for details.

B e d   &   B r e a k f a s t s

Concord Hill B&B • 473 Concord Hill Rd.
(314) 932-4228 • Rates: $75

Gramma's House B&B • 1105 Highway D
(314) 433-2675 • Rates: $75-105. Have stable accommodations for horses.

W i n e r y

Marthasville Vineyards, formerly Charrette Creek Winery
304 Depot Street (old MFA building) • Right on trail • (314) 433-5859

T here were fur traders and trappers in the area of La Charrette by the late 1700s. Daniel Boone's arrival in 1799 signified the continued approach of American colonization. When Lewis and Clark passed this way on their way west in 1804, this was the last white settlement they passed in Missouri.

The settlement at the site of present-day Marthasville was named for Dr. John Young's wife, Martha, in 1817. If you enjoy history, Marthasville will not disappoint. In 1835, Augustus Grabs built what is now the Grabs House Museum and Rusche Park. It began as a humble one-room log shoe shop. Mr. Grabs added to the building for residence, store and private school. Prearranged tours of the completely refurbished site are now available. St. Paul's United Church of Christ was established in 1863. The current church building atop "Church Hill" was dedicated in 1906.

In the downtown district, buildings are enriched with the Mesker Bros. metal facades (store fronts) and stories of ghosts in the old MKT boardinghouse.

Daniel Boone and his wife, Rebecca, were originally buried nearby on a tree-covered knoll overlooking Toque Creek. Their remains were subsequently removed to Frankfort, Kentucky in the 1840s. The monument at their original burial site stands as a tribute to the old Quaker.

Ask most locals, however, and you'll get a different story. Locals attest that the wrong body was pulled from its resting place and taken to Kentucky. According to one local, the exhumed body thought to be Daniel Boone was found to be the body of a black man, presumably that of Boone's lifelong friend and servant, who was buried next to him.

So where does the body of Daniel Boone now lie? Somewhere between the rolling hills of Kentucky and Missouri.

While Marthasville really is rich in history, it is also blessed with many fine business people who go out of their way to be helpful and friendly.

Scenic Cycles is truly a biker's oasis. In addition to repairing, selling and talking bikes, owners Terry and Cathy Turman also rent them. In addition to the usual mountain bike fare, rentals also include Burleys (kid carts) and Quadricycles, which are four-wheeled bikes that seat two and pedal and steer real easy.

Scenic Cycles say the Quadricycles are the perfect solution to those wanting to take their elderly or physically challenged friends out into the trail's outdoor bliss. Scenic Cycles also sells "PacDogs" and "Bobs," which are little trailers that can be pulled behind your bike.

The arrival of the Katy Trail in 1990 probably has revived Marthasville as much as the MK&T Railroad did almost a century earlier. Since the Katy Trail's completion in 1996, Marthasville residents have hosted many folks travelling long distances to ride and experience the Katy. Visitors have come from places as diverse as Austria, England, the Virgin Islands, Germany, Brazil, Australia and most corners of the United States.

Bikers' Note: Make sure your water bottles are filled in Marthasville. Good drinking water is not always readily available for long stretches.

Campers' Note: No campground currently exists in Marthasville. However, the Community Club often allows group camping near the pavilion. Call Don Sherman (in advance!) at (314) 433-2822. More primitive camping may become available during the 1997 season. Contact Scenic Cycles for more information.

How to Get to the Daniel Boone Monument: The monument is not visible from the trail. The Daniel Boone Monument is on . . . you guessed it . . . Daniel Boone Monument Road, which is a black top road that intersects the Katy Trail 1.5 miles east of Marthasville. Keep an eye out for the white house and tan shed off to the north of the trail.

Take this road north (towards the bluff). The road Ts within sight of the trail. Go left and follow the road 1.2 miles, and the monument is on the right. The monument is tucked in between cedar trees and old grave markers.

Washington

Food • Gas • Lodging • Post Office • Restrooms
Off the trail (other side of river, no walkway on bridge)
3 miles south of Dutzow and the trail, across the river on Highway 47
Washington Chamber of Commerce: (314) 239-2715
Post Office: (314) 239-3207 • Zip Code: 63090
From the Highway: From I-70 take Route 47 south, across the Missouri River.

This is the third and last town on the Katy Trail named after a president. Washington, population 11,367, has just about every service a trail user might need.

Bed & Breakfast
Schwegmann House Bed and Breakfast Inn
438 West Front Street • (314) 239-5025

Eastern Gray Tree Frog

Dutzow

Bikes • Food • Parking • Post Office • Restrooms • Winery
Milepost 74
3.7 miles from Marthasville to Dutzow • 7.7 miles from Dutzow to Augusta
Call Marthasville Chamber of Commerce for trail information:
(314) 433-5242 or Scenic Cycles at 433-2909
Post Office: (314) 433-2259 • Zip Code: 63342
From the Highway: From I-70, take Route 47 south to Route 94 east.

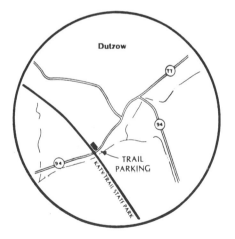

Dutzow

Eats

Charrette Creek Winery
304 Depot Street (old MFA building)
(314) 433-5859

Bicycle Rental

Charrette Creek Winery
304 Depot Street (old MFA building)
(314) 433-5859

Katy Bike Rental, Inc.
8080 Highway 94
(314) 433-KATY
Sat.-Sun. 10 a.m. - 6 p.m.

Winery

Blumenhof Vineyards and Winery
Right off Highway 94 • Accessible off of trail
(314) 433-2245

In 1824, a Rhinelander named Gottfried Duden arrived in Missouri and settled near present-day Dutzow. Four years later, he published a best-seller back in Germany, entitled *Report of a Journey to the Western States of North America*, in which he described the fertile Missouri River Valley and its likeness to southern Germany.

This glowing (and exaggerated) account inspired thousands of Germans to emigrate to the "New Rhineland." Settlement communities were organized. Both Hermann and Washington were founded by these settlement societies, and are still well known for their German culture and architecture. Here settlers could perpetuate their customs, handicrafts and hillside agriculture undisturbed by the tensions and strife that plagued the German states in the nineteenth century.

The town of Dutzow was established in 1833. In 1839, Jesuit priests came regularly to Dutzow, or Duseau as it was then called. Soon a parish was established and the first Saint Vincent de Paul Church was built in 1842. The railroad came through in the 1890s and the town prospered.

Augusta is home to wineries, antique shops and cat naps.

Augusta

Bikes • Crafts • Food • Lodging • Parking • Post Office • Restrooms • Wineries
Milepost 66
7.7 miles from Dutzow to Augusta • 5.7 miles from Augusta to Matson
Trail Info: (314) 228-4467 or 228-4464 • Visitors Association: (314) 228-4005
Post Office: (314) 228-4888 • Zip Code: 63332
Directions: From I-70, take 47 South to 94 East or 40/61 to Route 94 west.

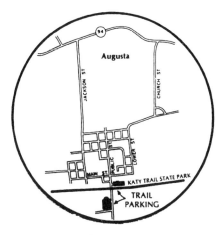

Augusta

E a t s

Bread Shed
5519 High Street

Cheese Wedge
5636 High Street

Katy Canteen
P.O. Box 73

Cookie Jar
5350 Hackman Road

Kountry Korner Breads
5625 High Street

Willow Bridge Restaurant and Bar
5350 Hackman Road

B e d   &   B r e a k f a s t s

Ashley's Rose Restaurant and Inn
5501 Locust
(314) 482-4108
Rates: $90

Lindenhof Country Inn
P.O. Box 52
(314) 228-4617

H.S. Clay House
Corner of Public and Walnut
P.O. Box 184 • (314) 482-4004
Rates: $105-145

B i c y c l e s

Touring Cyclist
5533 Water Street
(314) 228-4882

W i n e r i e s

Augusta Winery
Corner of High and Jackson Streets
(314) 228-4301

Mount Pleasant
Wine Company
5634 High Street
(314) 482-4419
1 (800) 467-WINE

Montelle Winery
Highway 94
(314) 228-4464

Jim Hartman, from Chicago, pedals across an impromptu finish line held by Carla Lang, of Boonville. The event marked the end of a five-day tour along the Katy Trail.

Remove the flashy new cars here in Augusta and any day in this town could pass for 1955 or even 1855. The town of Augusta is located atop gently rolling hills. A ride off the trail and up the winding road into town is a steep ride, but it's a definite must. Blooming dogwoods and redbud trees mix with the spring air to create an aura of another time.

Originally called Mount Pleasant, the town changed its name to Augusta when it applied for a post office and the name Mount Pleasant was already in use. The vineyards surrounding Augusta have been recognized for superior wine grapes since the 1800s. Augusta actually became America's first official wine district in 1880, because of the soil and the length of growing season within the 15-square-mile region.

The town was founded in 1836 by Leonard Harold, one of Daniel Boone's followers to St. Charles. The site was chosen for its excellent river landing. By incorporation in 1855, the town then known as Mount Pleasant had become predominantly German. These settlers were attracted by the glowing accounts of Gottfried Duden.

Until 1872, Augusta was a popular riverboat landing known as Augusta Bend. It was in this year that flooding of the Missouri River caused the river to fill in its main channel, changing its course and cutting Augusta off from the river. Fortunately for the town, the railroad was soon to follow.

As other towns have gone by the wayside, Augusta, with its 300 residents, is still a thriving small town. Much of the tourist interest, which was spurred by the revival of the vineyards in the late 1960s, has bloomed with the many homegrown businesses you see today. According to the locals, if a flag is flying near the door, you can be sure that business is open.

Enjoying Summer's Spell along the Katy Trail

The following article is based upon excerpts from Brett's journal while he was helping to lead a five-day tour of the Katy Trail during May 1996.

DAY ONE:

Touché! Touched down in Augusta, 5 p.m. Saturday, May 18th. Faded signs of ages past sizzle and sing on summer tin. Old brick storefronts reverberate with the massage of winds and energetic chirps from all kinds of tiny little birds. The song "Cat's in the Cradle with the Silver Spoon . . . " drifts up from an outdoor plaza where a one-man band does what one-man bands do.

I'm staying at Augusta's Ashley Rose B&B, as the sky tapers to tapestries aboard this gas of a first day on a weeklong tour of the Katy Trail, set up through Walt's Bicycle and Fitness in Columbia. I'm tooling along as the trip historian — a lunatic fringe visionary stuck in the past.

It was 95 degrees today as we left St. Charles, heading west across the bottoms toward our goal of reaching Sedalia, five days and close to 200 miles later. This summer may be the first season the entire 200 miles of the Katy Trail are open for riding. The finely packed trail surface makes for easy going, and despite a flat and a lot of seat adjusting, our first full day of riding passes without a hitch.

Our group is made up of old friends, who've grown close through countless rides and travels together. Most are from Chicago, with one couple from Columbia. Last summer they toured France's wine country by bike. This year, Darren Parker, the trip leader, and myself are proud to show them our own Rhineland, Missouri's burgeoning wine country.

Spring rains have finally subsided, leaving green saturated beauty hugging the trail as we go. The air hangs humid, but a gentle westerly breeze keeps the high temperatures from turning us to bacon. We drink water constantly, as the heat loosens our pores. Frequent breaks and a basket of strawberries provide a comfortable pace, as I tell the tale of Missouri's river valley and Darren follows nearby in the shuttle van.

As our first day teaches us, the predominant westerly winds would make a bike trip from Sedalia to St. Charles more bearable. These light breezes, though saving us from the heat, quickly sap our strength. There is no coasting today.

Day One we covered over 30 miles. Not bad considering this is the first ride this season's weather has permitted many of us. With a head wind, we averaged from 8 to 10 miles an hour. Without the wind, one could expect to comfortably log 12 to 15.

As we cool our heels now, freshly showered and relaxed from a comfortable day's ride, we look forward to an evening of fine food and wine, bed-and-breakfast style.

For, as our group learned last summer, biking is about more than pedaling. It's about arriving in new places, relishing things previously unseen. The Katy is the perfect path to unroll Missouri's welcome mat and show visitors how much our state has to offer.

Matson

Parking • Restrooms
Milepost 61
5.7 miles from Augusta to Matson • 1.5 miles from Matson to Defiance
From the Highway: From I-70, take Route 47 south to 94 East
or from St. Louis, take Highway 40/61 to Route 94 west.

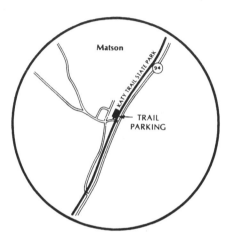

The area around Matson was originally settled by Daniel Boone in the early 1800s. Among the first settlers from Kentucky was Abraham Shobe. In 1819, he bought the original Daniel and Daniel Morgan Boone claims. When Shobe died in 1838, his grandson Abraham Matson bought the claims. And the rest is history.

In 1892, the Missouri-Kansas-Texas Railroad was opened through Matson. Richard Matson was instrumental in persuading the MK&T to build a station, water tank and coal chute in town in exchange for part of his land for a right-of-way. Several homes and a blacksmith shop were constructed and John Schermeier established a general store and post office.

Today, Matson doesn't offer much to the trail rider bent on racking up mileage at breakneck speeds. The town seems to be serenely slipping into history, like an old man on his rocker. There are a few backroads here that are screaming to be explored. The entrance to Sugar Creek Winery is right off the trail just west of Matson. The gorgeous view from the winery is well worth the steep climb.

Daniel Boone's home near Defiance, Missouri.

Defiance

Bikes • Food • Lodging • Parking • Post Office • Restrooms • Winery
Milepost 59
1.5 miles from Matson to Defiance • 3.1 miles from Defiance to Weldon Springs
Call The Trading Company of Defiance for trail information: (314) 987-2765
Post Office: (314) 987-2407 • Zip Code: 63341
From the Highway: From I-70, take Route 47 south to Route 94 east
or from St. Louis, take Highway 40/61 to Route 94 west.

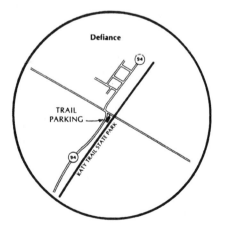

Eats

Defiance Inn
334 Old Colony Road
(314) 798-2300

The Trading Company of Defiance
2991 South Highway 94
(314) 987-2765

Terry & Betty's Tavern
P.O. Box 46
(314) 798-2441

Seasons & Memories
2886 South Highway 94
(314) 987-2203

Bicycle Rental

Katy Bike Rental
2998 South Highway 94
(314) 987-2673

Seasons & Memories
2886 South Highway 94
(314) 987-2203

Bed & Breakfasts

Das Gast Haus Nadler
Steps from the trail
125 Defiance Road
(314) 987-2200
Rates: $90 and up

Parson's House B&B
P.O. Box 38
211 Lee Street
(314) 798-2222
Rates: $70-90

The Country Porch B&B
15 Walnut Springs Drive
(314) 798-2546

Winery

Sugar Creek Winery
125 Boone Country Lane
(314) 987-2400

Defying History

Early settlers in the Defiance area were of English extraction, from either Virginia or Kentucky. In 1798, David Darst settled in the area, and Thomas and Phoebe Parsons purchased the claim of Joe Haynes (land grant number 14) in 1839. He built a brick house on the bluff, which is now the Parsons House B&B. The Parsons family owned most of the land where the town was built. James Craig, aware of the significance of the railroad to small towns, led a crusade to build a depot and a farm-to-market road (now Defiance Road). The town was then named Defiance because it had lured the railroad away from Matson in 1893.

The Schiermeier store here is worth a visit. It represents the totality of the interdependence between farmers and the railroad. The store sports two opposite-facing fronts. This boomtown phenomenon allowed one front to face the railroad, while the other front faced the farmers and local agriculture.

Daniel Boone in Missouri

Most Southerners are born knowing at least two lies: one about the Civil War and one about Daniel Boone.

In the absence of tangible records, some men's histories fade, while others find their way into the company of Gods. Oral history has kept the story of Daniel Boone alive, and today, through a strong mix of myth and fact, he has become one of America's best-known frontiersmen. He was a pioneer, scout, Indian fighter and trader.

Daniel Boone came to Missouri in 1799, after spending most of his life in North Carolina, Virginia, Kentucky and West Virginia. The Spanish government still controlled the Missouri country and Americans began to receive encouragement from Spain to cross the Mississippi and establish permanent settlements there. Daniel Boone was one of the first Americans to accept this invitation. He was appointed chief officer to the Femme Osage area in June of 1800. His duties included justice of the peace and militia commandant. He also divided up land for incoming pioneers.

He performed these duties from his home located in the Valley of Femme Osage near Defiance. Here Daniel and Rebecca settled after raising their eight children, a number that was common for the time. They also had 70 grandchildren and more than 250 great-grandchildren. His son Nathaniel (who incidentally had 14 children of his own) built the great stone house in Defiance.

Nearby is what some say is the famous "Judgment Tree" where Daniel conducted his court to settle disputes between white men and Native Americans. It was from here he wrote the following passage:

*I am hire With my hands full of Bisness and No athoraty,
and if I am Not indulged in What I Do for the best it Is Not
worth my While to put my Self to all this trubel . . .*

The house is still standing, only a few miles distant from the Katy Trail, and the grave sites of Daniel and his wife Rebecca are less than a mile off the route, just east of Marthasville. The house is furnished as it was when Daniel died on September 26, 1820.

In 1804, Nathaniel Boone and Tice Vanbibber had come upon a series of salt springs in a narrow valley in what is today Howard County. These would later become famous as Boone's Lick, near New Franklin and Boonville. This area became the destination of hundreds of emigrants drawn by little more than the promise of the Boone name. Today, the names of Boonville and Boone County echo the accomplishments of these early pioneers. Daniel Boone's home can be visited by calling (314) 987-2251. Or if you're within 25 miles in any direction, you can't miss the bright orange signs that lead you right to it. Gates close at 5 p.m. sharp, I found out, after arriving one day at 5 p.m. and 10 seconds.

Weldon Spring

Parking • Restrooms
Milepost 55
3.1 miles from Defiance to Weldon Spring
16.5 miles from Weldon Springs to St. Charles
Call the Trading Company of Defiance for trail information: (314) 987-2765
From the Highway: The Weldon Spring Conservation Area,
near the town of Weldon Spring, can be reached from
Highway 40/61 to 94 West to D or from Highway 70 to 94 to D.

Weldon Spring

If you're not expecting much when you get to the Weldon Spring trailhead, you won't be surprised. My first two questions were, "What services are here?" and "Can I ride by bike into Weldon Spring from the trailhead?"

A straight look and a "None and Nope" response were all it took to get me back on my bike seat. My first time through here was a bit of a shocker when I learned that the large ice-cold lemonade I'd been dreaming of was still four miles away. A large gravel parking lot doesn't make for a very climactic arrival, so you should schedule at the very least a small group of cheering friends or relatives to have a finish line pulled taut across the trail for you.

The trail doesn't even come close to Weldon Spring. What you are riding through is a large area that was recently incorporated by Weldon Spring. This part of the trail hugs the edge of the Missouri River and passes through some densely wooded areas across state-owned land. The actual town of Weldon Spring is located four miles northeast at the junction of Highways 94 and 40/61.

Just to the south you will pass a finely coated chert path that looks exactly like the Katy Trail until you start noticing WARNING signs posted every five feet on all sides. The government is in the process of cleaning up an old munitions plant where atom-bomb research was done during World War II. This area is like the cousin St. Louis doesn't want to talk about. If you're looking for a lengthy diversion, ask a local about the whole sordid story.

In addition to the 5.3 miles of the Katy Trail that pass through the Weldon Spring Conservation Area, there are several other trails nearby for hiking and biking. These include the 8-mile-long Lost Valley Trail (open only to hikers), the 8.2-mile-long Lewis Trail and the 5.3-mile-long Clark Trail. The St. Charles Convention and Visitors Bureau has free booklets highlighting these trails. Call them at (800) 366-2427 for a free copy. Ask for their other eco-guides, as well.

The history of this area is a prolific one. John Weldon came to this area in 1796 with a Spanish Land Grant for 425 acres, including the spring for which Weldon Spring was named. Nearly 150 years later, during World War II, the federal government acquired almost 17,000 acres in the area for the construction of a munitions plant. In 1948, the property (except for the munitions plant) was given to the University of Missouri for an agricultural experiment station.

The Conservation Department purchased 7,230 acres from the University in 1978. The acquisition brought the total contiguous acreage of Weldon Spring, Howell Island and August A. Busch Memorial Conservation Areas to 16,918 acres, 7,356 acres of which comprise Weldon Spring.

The area is rich in natural features. In addition to the Missouri River, with its rugged limestone cliffs, the area contains seven ponds, Femme Osage Slough and Prairie Lake.

Bikers' Note: Eight and a half miles west of St. Charles along the Katy Trail, at Pittmann Hill Road, BG&R Catering usually sets up a catering truck with food and drink from 10:30 a.m. to 3 p.m. on good weather days.

St. Charles

Bikes • Camping • Casino • Crafts • Food • Gas • Hostel • Lodging
Microbrewery • Parking • Restrooms • RV hookups
Milepost 39
16.5 miles from Weldon Springs to St. Charles
12 miles from St. Charles to Machens
Visitors Center: (314) 946-7776 or 1 (800) 366-2427
Post Office: (314) 724-4810 • Zip Codes: 63301, 63302, 63303, 63304
From the Highway: Take I-70 to St. Charles Fifth Street exit. Go north to
Boonslick Road and turn right. Take Boonslick to Riverfront Drive and park.

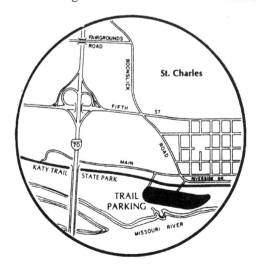

St. Charles

E a t s

Big A's On the Riverfront
308 North Main Street

Boccacio's Restaurant
820 South Main Street

Café Beignet
515 South Main

Lewis and Clark's
217 South Main

Little Hills Winery
501 South Main

Magpie Café
524 South Main

Old Mill Stream Inn
912 South Main

River Star Café
117 South Main

Riverside Restaurant & Bar
204 North Main

St. Charles Vintage House
1219 South Main

The Copper Platter
625 South Main

The Lindsey Gardner House
803 South Main

Noah's Ark
I-70 & Fifth Street

The Pub
221 North Main

B e d   &   B r e a k f a s t s

Boone's Lick Trail Inn
1000 South Main
(314) 947-7000
Rates: $85-135

Historic Main B&B
423 South Main
(314) 940-8847
Rates: $90-130

Lady B's B&B
631 North Benton
(314) 947-3421
Rates: $55-85

Loccoco House II B&B
1309 North Fifth
(314) 946-0619
Rates: $75

Sage House B&B
1717 Elm Street
(314) 947-4843
Rates: $65-85

St. Charles House Elegant B&B
338 South Main
(314) 946-6221
Rates: $105-140

H o s t e l

Lewis & Clark International Hostel • On I-70 at Zumbehl and Highway 94
2750 Plaza Way • (314) 949-8700
24-hour registration. Airport Pickup, 7 a.m. - 9 p.m.

Lodging

St. Charles also has 11 hotels. The Budgetel located at 1425 S. 5th Street, (314) 946-6936, is a favorite of many bikers. Contact the St. Charles Visitors Center at 1 (800) 366-2427, at 230 South Main Street, for more information.

RV Parks & Campgrounds

Sundermeier RV Park • 111 Transit St. • (314) 940-0111 or 1 (800) 929-0832 Only RV park in St. Charles • Full hookups • Laundry • Hot Showers • Camping. Go Highway 94 north at 2nd Street to 2000 block, right on Transit, 2 blocks.

Twin Island Lake • 7375 Highway 40-61 • (314) 447-0011

Bicycle Rental

Katy Bike Rental
1038 South Main
(314) 949-6800

Touring Cyclist
104 South Main
(314) 949-9630

Riverboats

Casino St. Charles
1260 S. Main Street
(314) 947-3323

Goldenrod Showboat
Showboat Landing
(314) 946-2020

St. Charles

A visit to downtown St. Charles, which was once the capital of Missouri, feels like walking into a historical photo. The cobblestone of Main Street works its rhythm beneath your feet as you stroll past antique shops and ice-cream parlors along this friendly 10-block corridor into the past. Pass the afternoon in the shade, walk the trail or join in a game of frisbee down by the river.

The activity in St. Charles doesn't set with the sun, so if you're not in a hurry, try your luck on one of the riverboat casinos docked within walking distance of the trail or dine outside at one of the many tempting restaurants and cafés nearby.

Founded as Les Petites Cotes (The Little Hills) by French Canadian fur trader Louis Blanchette in 1769, this area became the headquarters for the fur trading industry along the Missouri River. By 1791, the population had grown to 255 and the second Catholic church, replacing Blanchette's first one (1769), was dedicated under the invocation to San Carlos Borromeo (1538-1584), archbishop of Milan and patron saint of Charles IV, King of Spain. On the day the church was dedicated, the town changed its name to San Carlos. San Carlos was "americanized" to St. Charles in 1804 during the formalization of the Louisiana Purchase. In subsequent years, St. Charles, like many other Missouri towns, was greatly affected by western expansion, German immigration (beginning in the 1830s), the 1849 California Gold Rush, the railroad and river trade.

Before Missouri was granted statehood in 1821, various locations had served as the government seat for territorial affairs. As statehood became a certainty, the permanent site of Jefferson City was chosen. But until the new Capitol could be constructed, nine cities vied for the honor of hosting the state's temporary seat of government. The citizens of St. Charles furnished free meeting space for the legislators and won the honor.

continued on page 140

Be prepared for spontaneous relaxation.

The St. Charles' Tourism Center is a good place to find out about the many outdoor concerts and events scheduled for the summer.

The state's first legislators met here from June 1821 through October 1826, when the new Capitol was ready for use in Jefferson City. The Missouri Department of Natural Resources gives tours of the fully restored first Capitol, where frontiersmen and scholars alike met atop the Peck Brothers General Store. Tours are available Monday through Saturday every hour. The First Missouri State Capitol is located at 200 S. Main. Call for more information, (314) 946-9282.

The Lewis and Clark Museum is also worth a look. This trading post is filled with the unusual Indian artwork they found during their travels. It is located at 701 Riverside Drive or call (314) 947-3199 for tour information. There is also an old train depot here that was restored by the city before the trail was opened. Although it's not part of the trail corridor, the depot is usually open to the public.

There are many other interesting structures throughout town, as well. In the basement of 318 South Main Street there are bars on the windows and pegs in the wall because this is where the first state prison was located. The house at 724 South Main Street was the presidential campaign headquarters for Abraham Lincoln. The St. Charles Convention and Visitors Bureau has several tour brochures, one on South Main Street and one on French Town, located farther east.

Annual events include the Lewis and Clark Rendezvous the third weekend of May; the Festival of the Little Hills the third weekend in August; Ragfest each Labor Day; a bluegrass festival each September; and the Missouri River Storytelling Festival and Oktoberfest each October. Contact the St. Charles Visitors Center, 230 South Main Street, at 1 (800) 366-2427, for information on special events. Look for a free copy of *Cycle St. Louis* at the Touring Cyclist bike shop on South Main for maps of nearby moutain biking trails and biking events.

Machens

No services
Milepost 27
12 miles from St. Charles to Machens

As of March 1997, the Katy Trail ended in St. Charles. Plans to continue the trail east of St. Charles to Machens are still stymied due to three large sink holes caused by the 1993 flood. The Department of Natural Resources is negotiating with nearby landowners for possible easements so the trail can be relocated. This part of the trail may be completed by the end of the 1997 season. Check with the Department of Natural Resources for up-to-date information.

Machens was first settled in the late 1700s by the Payne family. Henry Machens brought his family here in 1848 and worked hard to bring the railroad to town.

Here, the 55-foot replica of the Lewis and Clark keelboat, constructed by Glen Bishop of St. Charles, passes through a desolate stretch along the Missouri River.

The Corps of Discovery, Then and Now

At the bequest of Thomas Jefferson, Meriwether Lewis and William Clark were commissioned to explore the recently acquired Louisiana Purchase in 1804. Their mission was to search for an overland waterway to the Pacific, map the newly acquired territory, study the flora and fauna and establish relations with the many Native American tribes along the way.

Lewis and Clark's 7,000-mile journey took them from the confluence of the Mississippi and Missouri Rivers near St. Louis, across the Rockies and to the Pacific Ocean. Upon returning to St. Louis two years and four months later, they found they had been assumed dead. They were met with great fanfare. Many still call this the most successful military expedition ever undertaken. With grueling conditions, fierce winters and rugged terrain, the crew still only lost one member — due to appendicitis.

When the Corps of Discovery left in May of 1804, the first 500 miles of the voyage was through present-day Missouri.

The year 2004 will be a festive one in St. Louis. This year will mark the bicentennial of the Lewis and Clark Expedition and the 100-year anniversary of the World's Fair of 1904. Already, billboards dot the St. Louis cityscape, offering in two-foot-high letters the dictum "THINK 2004."

Crew members (left to right), James Felder, Capt. Glen Bishop, W. Crosby Brown and Bob Plummer search for the next mile marker to compare with their navigation charts.

Shadows of Heroes Past
Expedition Traces Route of Lewis and Clark

Aboard the Discovery Expedition reenactment, timelines blur between 1804 and present day. Capt. Glen Bishop of St. Charles and a diehard crew of fellow modern-day adventurers are retracing Lewis and Clark's epic search for an inland water route to the Pacific, which began in 1804.

On stretches of the river where Lewis and Clark would have poled their keelboat upriver in three feet of water on a river a mile wide, today's bottlenecked channel runs 30 feet deep or more. As the river rises, its speed increases, making our inboard motor a welcome historical anachronism.

This voyage began 12 years ago, as Bishop, a curious carpenter and stained glass business owner, began piecing together a replica of Lewis and Clark's 55-foot keelboat in his backyard. He used sketches from Clark's journal as his guide.

After crafting a 55-inch model of the keelboat in 1984, he built the full-scale reproduction that earned First Place awards in the Washington, D.C., Independence Day Parade in 1992.

In 1996, the Discovery Expedition stopped in 21 towns along the Missouri River, covering more than 450 nautical miles as the boat journeyed from the state's eastern edge in St. Charles to its western slope at St. Joseph.

"This is a sorta test-drive for 2004," says Bishop, referring to the year of the Lewis and Clark bicentennial.

Bishop's ability to deemphasize the epic scale of this trip has been key to the trip's success. The fluid nature of the trip's logistics demands such a careful aloofness as weather, river, boat and human factors continually change.

Plans for 1997 include a trip down the Ohio River from where the original keelboat was constructed, with subsequent years seeing other legs of the original Discovery Expedition reenacted.

The keelboat replica is a testament to the skills and determination of Glen, and the support of his wife, Joanne, family, friends, and fellow residents of St. Charles, Missouri.

For more information on future keelboat projects, call the Greater St. Charles Convention and Visitors Center at (314) 946-7776 or visit online at discovery.showmestate.com. The boat and its modern-day crew are also featured in the book, *River Revisited – In the Wake of Lewis and Clark,* available from Pebble Publishing.

Bob Plummer, from Hermann, gives the full ahead sign as he watches for uprooted trees in the current. Largely submerged, the uprooted trees float towards the wood-hulled keelboat like lumbering landmines.

Visiting St. Louis

St. Louis is located about 20 minutes northeast of St. Charles
St. Louis Convention and Visitors Bureau: (314) 421-1023 or 1 (800) 325-7962

St. Louis has it all, from jazz and the Arch to the St. Louis Science Center. If you are weary and worn after finishing your 200-mile trek here, it is the perfect place to indulge every desire the modern world can provide. If you are interested in visiting St. Louis while at this end of the trail, there are many sites worth exploring. They are mentioned here briefly to help you plan your stay. A complete listing of B&Bs, restaurants and other services is available from the Visitors Center, listed above.

Anheuser-Busch Tour Center — Visit the famous Clydesdale horses, the aging rooms and the packaging plant and enjoy free, cold beer. No tours on Sunday. I-55 and Arsenal Street. (314) 577-2626.

Bowling Hall of Fame and Museum — Offers "a world of fascinating facts and history. Get tips from masters and play on futuristic lanes." (314) 231-6340.

Cahokia Mounds — In Illinois, just across the river from St. Louis lies the largest prehistoric Native American city north of Mexico. On 2,200 acres, there are 68 mounds and an interpretive center bringing this culture from 850 A.D. back to life. Three miles west of Collinsville on Collinsville Road, Illinois. (618) 346-5160.

There are three *casinos* in St. Louis — Casino Queen, 200 S. Front Street East, 1 (800) 777-0777; the President Casino, St. Louis Levee, below the Arch, 1 (800) 772-3647; and the Casino St. Charles, 1260 S. Main Street, (314) 947-3323.

The Dog Museum — Dedicated to preserving the arts, artifacts and literature about man's best friend. (314) 821-3647.

Gateway Arch — Gateway to the West, at 630 feet tall, is the tallest man-made monument in the nation. A tram inside takes you to the top (where it sways back and forth) giving a great view of the city and the Mississippi River. Jefferson National Expansion Memorial. (314) 425-4465.

Jefferson Barracks — These five buildings make up this influential and historic military base, active for 120 years between 1826 and 1946. South end of Broadway off Kingston Road. (314) 544-5714.

Laclede's Landing — This revitalized historic river district is north of the Arch (between Eads and King Bridges). It combines cobblestone streets with shops, cafés, bars and clubs.

Mercantile Money Museum — Presents the history and oddities of money through displays and exhibits. Free. (314) 421-1819.

Missouri Botanical Garden — The Missouri Botanical Garden is a collection of interesting flower and plant displays, including the world's first geodesic dome and the largest traditional Japanese garden in North America. Wander through the rose garden or tropical rainforest. 4344 Shaw Avenue. (314) 577-5100.

Museum of Transportation — 150 years of history, including locomotives, vintage autos, aircraft and riverboats. 3015 Barrett Station Road. (314) 965-7998.

National Expansion Memorial — Highlighting our country's westward expansion. Located below the Arch. This is a must see.

Riverboat McDonald's — How can you resist? Eat a Big Mac on the Mighty Mississippi, within sight of the Arch. Open daily. (314) 231-6725.

Six Flags Over America — Southwest on I-44, Exit 261. (314) 938-4800.

St. Louis Art Museum — Collections range from ancient to contemporary. One Fine Arts Drive. (314) 721-0072.

St. Louis Cathedral — A mix of Byzantine interior and Romanesque exterior, featuring a 22-story-high dome. Inside you'll also find one of the biggest mosaic collections in the world. 4431 Lindell Boulevard. (314) 533-0544.

St. Louis Science Center — Hundreds of interactive exhibits including an Omnimax Theater, a planetarium and full-size animated battling dinosaurs. 5050 Oakland Avenue. (314) 289-4444.

St. Louis Union Station — Shopping, dining, history, lodging and entertainment. Open daily. 1820 Market Street, between 18th and 20th Streets. (314) 421-6655.

The Magic House and *St. Louis Children's Museum* — This place is a blast! Located in a 3-story Victorian mansion, the Magic House has hands-on interactive exhibits in magic, astronomy, gravity, physics, light, mazes and more. It makes learning a great way to spend the day.

Amtrak Train Terminal, 550 S. 16th Street, 1 (800) 872-7245
Greyhound Bus, 1450 N. 13th Street, 1 (800) 231-2222
Lambert–St. Louis International Airport, (314) 426-8000
MetroLink, urban train network, weekdays 10 a.m. - 3 p.m. (314) 231-2345
Parks and Recreation, (314) 889-2863
Public Transportation: Bi-State Transit (314) 231-2345
Taxi cabs: County 991-5300; Laclede 652-3456; Yellow 361-2345
Time and Temperature 321-2522; **Weather Line** 321-2222

GETTING
—— FROM A TO B ——

Missouri's Amtrak

The Amtrak train is a smart way to return to your beginning point if you have ridden the entire Katy Trail. Unreserved one-way between K.C. and St. Louis is about $53. There are frequent stops in many towns across the state. Hermann, Jefferson City and Sedalia are the most accessible from the trail. Unfortunately, you CANNOT bring your bike aboard the train. I eventually called the D.C. headquarters of Amtrak to explain how ridiculous this was. A guy named Mark summed it up: "It's a bad scene. They can't get their bike on the train even if they throw a fit. Only folding bicycles are accepted."

The Amtrak passenger line was, as Mark put it, "hanging on by its fingernails," when the state of Missouri financed the operation of the train to keep it going. Since it has a bare-bones budget, there aren't any baggage handlers at any of the stops, making it IMPOSSIBLE to bring a bike aboard. You are allowed two carry-on bags, however. Believe me, I tried every bike scenario and Amtrak had a bylaw prohibiting every outlandish scheme. Here's what you can ask to determine whether your particular line carries bikes: "Does the train between point A and B have check baggage (called AB space)?" If so, you can buy a box from Amtrak for $7 and take the bike with you. If you want to ride the train, another option would be to have a trailhead bike shop box up your bike and ship it home. You might call Touring Cyclist in St. Charles or BikeWerks in Sedalia for more information.

If this puts a prickle in your vacation plans, call Amtrak Custom Vacations at 1 (800) 321-8684 or ask for their customer relations number in D.C. For more information on Amtrak routes, try them online at http://www.amtrak.com.

FOR MORE INFORMATION CALL 1 (800) USA-RAIL

— *Greyhound* —

G reyhound Bus Lines do allow you to take your bike with you, as long as it is broken down and in a box. They charge an extra $10 for this service and you'll have to round up your own box from a nearby bike shop. You are also permitted two carry-ons.

Greyhound has four daily buses running hither and yon around Missouri. Kansas City to St. Charles one-way is $35. St. Louis to Columbia (midpoint of trail) is about $25. Greyhound only stops in those towns along the Interstate 70 highway corridor, making the best points of bus departure for trail users to be: Boonville, Columbia, St. Charles and St. Louis. Remember: If you are in Sedalia, or between McBaine and Weldon Springs, you are far away from I-70 and Greyhound's bus stops. Call 1 (800) 231-2222 for more information.

Sore Butt Shuttles

D espite all of the development along the trail, there still isn't an all-encom-passing shuttle service. The most frequent questions I get regard shuttle service and camping.

I recently talked to a man planning to fly his family into K.C. to take a week and ride the Katy Trail. "How do I get from K.C. to Sedalia?" he asked, a distance of 60 miles. A taxi would be too expensive. So do you rent a car? There seems to be no real answer.

Since this is the biggest hitch in many people's vacations, I, as well as a few other businesses along the trail, are now providing limited shuttle service on a come-and-go basis. If you are realizing this hitch in your plans, or simply need a shuttle back to your car at the other end of the trail, or even just a 15-20 mile return trip, call one of the numbers listed below. Also, **Bikers' Notes** in each town list some other options for getting across bridges and from point A to point B. One final note: When planning your week sojourn, please call ahead and confirm dates and times. These people won't always be available at the last minute.

Call Sore Butt Shuttles at 1 (800) 576-7322 and ask for Brett. We'll figure out a solution to your travel needs and take it from there.

Or try Cathy Turman at Scenic Cycles, 203 Depot Street, Marthasville, MO. (314) 433-2909. In addition to renting, selling and repairing bikes, she offers a driver/shuttle service. She will transport riders in their own cars to where they want to start riding. Then she will drive their cars to the end destination and park it. This must be planned in advance. Call for details.

Campground Quick Reference Guide

T hroughout this book, if there is any sort of camping available, there are **Campers' notes** at the end of each section. Unlike many well-established rails-to-trails across the country, the Katy Trail is very young, which results in a shortage of needed services, primarily camping and lodging. The most frequently asked question I get is camping! Well, there's not much of it. Sedalia, Columbia and Hermann offer public campgrounds.

If you are looking for family-oriented camping, I recommend the Katy Round-house in the New Franklin area, Sundermeier RV Park in St. Charles and calling Steve Hunt in Portland, at (573) 676-5396, to see what he has cooking.

If you move from the strictest definition of campground and are looking for nothing more than a flat spot to pitch a tent, there are several places along the trail that could offer a small patch of grass.

The best piece of advice is ASK. There are usually people around willing to let a biker or a couple of hikers camp out for the night. See **Bikers' Bulletin Board** for additional ideas.

New Franklin
Katy Roundhouse Campground. The Katy Roundhouse also rents bikes, tents and has showers and a nice restaurant. Trail Mile Marker 189 (1893 Katy Drive). (816) 848-2232

Easley
Michael Cooper's place can't be beat. It's RIGHT on the river. Camping is primi-tive, with water, and access to the store's bathroom and shower during open hours. (573) 657-2544

Bluffton
Rendleman Home Bed & Breakfast. The Rendlemans' B&B has camping spaces available for up to 10 people. They've put in two bathrooms in their barn, behind their B&B, and hope to have a kitchen completed upstairs in the barn by summer. Call ahead for more information. (573) 236-4575

St. Charles — Not on trail
Twin Island Lake. 7375 Highway 40-61. (314) 447-0011. 50 acres. Fishing, swim-ming, camping.

Sundermeier's RV Park
Just east of where the current trailhead stops in St. Charles. Probably one of truest "campgrounds" along the trail. Camping area, hot showers and clean bathrooms.

Campground Quick Reference Guide

Other suggestions:

Other than the aforementioned campgrounds, other camping options along the trail are very primitive – not what you're looking for after driving 12 hours with several young children.

The following suggestions should be taken as such. These are LEADS and in no way imply that you'll find anything at all when you pull through town. So many of these businesses are at the whim of the weather and the fluctuating river, that their plans early in the year may be very different than what they offer later in the season.

Wilton
Riverview Traders Restaurant & General Store. Right across from the trail. Primitive camping and tipi camping may become available sometime in 1997. Call for more information: (573) 657-1095.

Tebbetts
The Turner's Store. Mrs. Turner SOMETIMES lets polite and courteous trailusers camp next door. Past grain elevators, next to the post office. (573) 295-6112.

Steedman
Sometimes people camp in the grassy area in front of S.O.B.'s. Ask for permission at the bar. No bathroom.

Portland
A lot of people pitch a tent at the riverfront. No services. Follow the river access road to get there.

Resident Steve Hunt is also planning to operate a campground in Portland beginning in the spring of 1997. This campground is 2 blocks north of the trail by the Episcopalian church. He is planning to have showers, bathrooms, bike rental and sales. He also plans to have group camping areas and picnic tables. He also mentioned interest in helping bikers with shuttles on a part-time basis. Before setting arrival dates and hard-to-meet expectations, call Steve for the complete lowdown to confirm what services are available: (573) 676-5396.

Bikers Bulletin Board

These observations were culled from comments and advise from fellow hikers, bikers and online responses to several forums on the *Interactive Katy Trail*. May they aid you in planning your next adventure!

There isn't much shade between **Hartsburg** and **Jefferson City**. • The **bluffs** along Rocheport, Jefferson City and near Bluffton are definite highlights of the ride. • October was proclaimed Katy Trail State Park month by Governor Mel Carnahan. • **Cooper's Landing**: The owner was hospitable and flexible, as we arrived late. He enabled us to show up and camp and continue to enjoy our trip. • **Augusta**: The Cookie Jar (up the hill) is the only restaurant open at 7 a.m. Great breakfast! • **St. Charles**: Java, Jazz and Blues has live bands every night except Monday. Very pleasant owners who educated us to the great varieties of coffee. Best shake (with a shot of expresso) I've ever experienced! Corey S. • Great, friendly people throughout the trail. Very helpful. John • Ride North Jefferson to **Tebbetts** in the a.m. It's a long ride. No services in between. Pack plenty of water. • **New Franklin** to Rocheport is a long, hot ride. Pack plenty of water. • After every door closed on us for **camping** we spent a night in a hotel in **Jefferson City** and headed home the next day. Have you ever biked the Sparta to Elroy trail Wisconsin? We did last year and camped at a beautiful campground right off the trail. I guess that's what we were expecting for the Katy Trail. Maybe our expectations are premature since the trail is only 2 years old. Let us know when campgrounds are more developed—with showers and toilets suitable for families with young children. • Coming from the west, don't take the first exit at **Boonville**. It takes you too far into town where there aren't many services. Instead, go to where it dead-ends at the bridge. Then cross over the **bridge** to New Franklin. • The trip was a great time and a must for those who like to tour the outdoors. M. Albright. • **Trailhead Brewery** in St. Charles is not very courteous or polite. • **Dotty's Café** in Hartsburg served incredible breakfast. • Take a hammock or a sheet! Gregg B. • I rode the new **Columbia extension** from McBaine to both Columbia and Rocheport. This is a great addition to the trail and allows Columbia residents to have immediate access to the Katy. I also rode the **Jefferson City extension** which is now open. They have a huge covered picnic area, bathrooms and sinks with running water, water fountains and a water faucet to fill water bottles. If they add a telephone and a soda machine, we will just about have it all. • While the twin **Jefferson City bridges** don't have a bike lane, with three lanes each, it is relatively safe to ride across them as long as it is not rush hour. • It does not appear the **Easley** store is going to reopen at all. • **Mokane** is not someplace you want to leave your vehicle, especially overnight. The local boys like to trash them. I would also be concerned in areas where farmers fought the trail like **Portland** and **Rhineland**. David S. • Some friends of mine came to ride the entire trail. They had trouble finding a place to **camp** and more importantly getting showers and water. • To stay in **B&Bs** along the trail, make sure and call well before arriving. During the peak months, **many are filled by reservations a month or two in advance**. • **Air up your tires** to maximum psi or put road tires on your MTB.

Snakes! You may see them while on your trip. They use the trail too. Oftentimes, they are heading across the trail, which stretches them out to their full length. Do not throw rocks at them or kill them intentionally. They are peaceful creatures and should not be messed with. Several Missouri snakes have inflammatory bites, so keep your distance. • **Near Cedar City / Jefferson City:** Taking advantage of the facilities at the airport allows you to avoid riding into Jefferson City across the Missouri River. Just .5 mile from the shelter east over the 54 Overpass on Highway W is the **Jefferson City Memorial Airport**. It is open extended hours from 6 a.m. to sunset daily. It has the following facilities year-round: pay telephone (outside on the south side of the building), heated restrooms, water, Catoan's Restaurant, (573) 635-5698, (good!); and Hertz Rent-A-Car, (573) 761-3535. Expect more extended hours in the summer months. Info courtesy of Dave Smallwood. Thanks Dave! • **Scenic Cycles** is a bikers' oasis. They are in Marthasville.

Proposed Routes and Trips

A leisurely afternoon jaunt for great chow and a view of the bluffs can begin and end in **Hartsburg**. Eat at **Dotty's Café**, where lunch specials are usually less than $5 (including drink). The restaurant is very wheelchair accessible. • Stop in **Rocheport** for lunch and a saunter along the trail. Or eat lunch, rent a bike and check out the train tunnel to the west and the gorgeous bluffs and view of the river to the east. • Make sure to be in St. Charles the third weekend in May for the annual **Lewis and Clark Rendezvous.** • An aggressive **four day ride** will allow you to see the whole trail. This ride was planned by Frank Wyatt, Darnell Harris and Mark Neagli of Houston, Texas. Day 1: Sedalia to Rocheport (49 miles) • Day 2: Rocheport to Bluffton (68 miles) • Day 3: Bluffton to Defiance (51 miles) • Day 4: Defiance to St. Charles (short day)

Gastronomic Highlights

There is one thing better than riding the Katy Trail — eating along the Katy Trail. The following are suggestions to slow the pace of your pedal and widen your waist: Cobbler and real mash potatoes at Dotty's Café in Hartsburg • Trailside Café's buffalo burgers and tenderloins • Hamburgers and chili dogs at Betty's Bar and Grill in McBaine • Dessert at the Word Of Mouth Café in Rocheport • Wine and a basket of meat and cheese at any winery along the trail

Scout Outing Notes

See **Campers' Notes** • Nick Cipponeri, of the **Windhomme Hill B&B** near **Treloar** is a gourmet chef. He often does catering to groups along the trail and offers candlelight dinners occasionally. He also offers weekend cooking classes. Call for more info: 1 (800) 633-0582 and (314) 932-4234. • Though camping is not currently allowed in the town of **Rocheport** proper, scouting groups are often allowed to set up near trailside businesses. Call for more information: (573) 698-2702. **Group camping** is also available in Marthasville. Call Scenic Cycles at (314) 433-2822 or see the **Marthasville Campers' note** for more information.

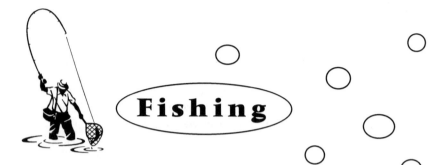

Fishing

Fishing is a logical way to further one's enjoyment along this natural corridor. A biker or hiker could easily take along 50 feet of 30-pound test line, some 1-ounce sinkers and some number 4 hooks and turn any ordinary afternoon into a small fishing expedition.

The flood of '93 cleansed out the river considerably and many people can be seen fishing up and down the Missouri. In addition to fishing the river, many have taken to seeking their bounties in the many recently formed "blue hole" lakes.

The Missouri River is host to several dozen kinds of fish. There are blue cat, white cat, channel cat, flathead, spoonbill, sturgeon, drum, eel, carp, buffalo, sauger and suckers. Near streams, you may also find bass, perch, crappie and walleye.

The first step toward making your river fishing trip a positive one is to leave your lightweight fishing rods and tackle at home. A strong river requires a strong rod or stick. The 30-pound test fishing line is recommended more for fighting snags than walleye. There are plenty of places along the river to get bait and a fishing license.

You can unspool your line and bank fish with a sturdy stick or "limb fish" from a hearty limb. Heavy sinkers allow the line to bury itself in the mud and a good 18-inch leader will allow your bait to float in the current. And be ready — just about anything could come out of that river. . . .

Fishing Access Points

DEPARTMENT OF CONSERVATION
MISSOURI RIVER ACCESS AREAS

AREA	RIVER	COUNTY	FACILITIES
Blanchette Landing	Missouri	St. Charles	P, Cr, HT
Chamois	Missouri	Osage	P, Cr
Cooley Lake C.A.	Missouri	Clay	P, Cr
Franklin Island	Missouri	Howard	P, Cr, T
Hartsburg	Missouri	Boone	P, Cr, T
Hermann	Missouri	Gasconade	P, Cr, HT, HJ
Hoot Owl Bend	Missouri	Atchison	P
Howell Island	Missouri	St. Charles	P
Langdon Bend	Missouri	Atchison	P, Cr, T
Marion	Missouri	Cole	P, Cr, T
Miami Rvrfrnt Prk	Missouri	Saline	P, Cr, T
Mokane	Missouri	Callaway	P, Cr, T
New Haven	Missouri	Franklin	P, Cr
Nodaway Island	Missouri	Andrew	P, Cr, T
Paynes Landing	Missouri	Holt	P, Cr, T
Taylor's Landing	Missouri	Cooper	P, Cr, T
Thurnau C.A.	Missouri	Holt	P, Cr, T
Washington Park	Missouri	Franklin	P, Cr
Weldon Springs	Missouri	St. Charles	P, Cr, T
Worthwine Island	Missouri	Andrew	P

TRIBUTARIES

Coulter's Landing	Boeuf Creek	Franklin	P, Cr, T
Capitol View	Cedar Creek	Callaway	P, Cr, HT
Piggs Landing	Fishing	Ray	P, Cr, T
Moreau-50	Moreau	Cole	P, Cr, T
Watson	Nishnabotna	Atchison	P, Cr, T
Bonnots Mill	Osage	Osage	P, Cr, T
Providence	Perche Creek	Boone	P, Cr, T

Facilities Key

P - parking lot (gravel)
Cr - concrete ramp
T - toilet
HT - handicapped-accessible toilet
HJ - handicapped-accessible jetty

The Flood of '93

The dome of the Capitol building in Jefferson City became two, as flooded streets mirrored the skyline above and continued to rise . . . as fast as 9 feet in 24 hours.

As the Waters Recede

By Michelle E. Moore

❖

It began softly, slowly, almost like a whisper. First a light patter, just enough to turn the concrete from flaxen dust to a healthy beige. Soon neighbors couldn't remember the last dry day. They watched their grass grow sober and straight and packed the lawnmower away for another not-so-soggy day.

But the skies kept unfolding.

For most, the sound of rain against the rooftop became as routine as the sun's warmth that once seeped through bedroom curtains in the morning. The television showed water edging intimately into backyards that looked far too familiar.

Those closest to the rising currents traded umbrellas for heavy work boots, soles caked perpetually with mud. We called it Lake Missouri, shook our heads and laughed, because that's all some of us could muster.

We cursed the swollen river, the northern skies for dumping more rain near the Mississippi, our sky for the pounding sun, the burden of the sandbags. Many of us could only grieve, huddled over a few precious possessions packed into a pickup bed.

When summer crept into fall, we found the surface of our communities changed. The trees. Gone. The animals. Gone. Bridges. Gone. The house next door. Gone. And the sand, the mud, the corpses, pieces of a highway, pieces of our lives, wherever the water let them lie. Here.

The Hartsburg bottoms were scoured and covered with sand.

From left, Hartsburg-area farmers Wayne Hilgedick, Orion Beckmeyer and Missouri Farm Bureau's Charles Kruse listen as Gen. Gerald Galloway, a White House representative, says he'll look into levee repair.

Nature Rolls the Dice

By Brett Dufur
Columbia Missourian

McBAINE — Some river gamblers don't dress in fancy tuxedos. Dusty boots and overalls are their attire. The dice they throw is seed. The dealer: Mother Nature herself.

The majority of river bottom farmers will take the gamble and plant this spring, despite sand and breached levees that remain from last year's flood. Others are too busy working on levees and reclaiming land to give planting much thought.

"We still don't have any official word from the Corps of Engineers," said Wayne Hilgedick, a Hartsburg farmer with more than 11,000 acres. "We're not going to bet on having the levees back up this season. We're just going to have to take a gamble." He hopes to plant from 80 to 90 percent of his land.

"You have to be a gambler," said Glen Beckmeyer of Hartsburg. "I've been gambling ever since I started farming here in 1980. Sometimes you lose, but then again sometimes you win, too."

By invitation, a White House representative visited the bottoms on March 23, 1994. Despite numbing winds, Gen. Gerald Galloway, chairman of the Flood Plain Management Review Committee, talked for an hour with 10 Hartsburg and McBaine farmers.

Reassured that help was on the way, the farmers returned to their tractors to work the sand-swept land.

"There are levee repairs going as fast as possible," Galloway said.

Many have heard enough talk. "The money has been appropriated. So why is the Corps of Engineers still sitting on their hands? This is ridiculous," said Paul Hibbard, a flood coordinator for the Secretary of Agriculture. "With the education they've got, they should have some answers.

"This is the bread basket of the world. We should be getting the job done," he said.

Because levees fall under federal, state and local ownership, levee repair has turned into a disjointed logistical nightmare — a myriad of individualized solutions.

Many farmers have resorted to repairing gaping holes with their own tractors because federal help has been slow. Much of the sand is used to fill in holes cut by the river's force. The rest is either spread around to disperse it, or bulldozed into corners.

Large metal discs pulled by a tractor turn the mix practically upside down, leaving the soil on top. But several feet of sand requires larger discs and more horsepower to pull them.

"We used two scrapers with a four-wheel-drive tractor, but it's hard to get traction in sand," said John Sam Williamson, a farmer with 1,100 acres in the McBaine bottoms, who will lose about 100 acres of crop production due to sand and holes. "We might need a bigger tractor, or one that drives on wide rubber tracks."

In accordance with federal levee repair regulations, Hartsburg farmers are repairing 20 percent of the levee, building up one end of the levee with their own tractors. It's uncertain when the federal government will repair the remainder.

Clifton Nahler's approach kills two birds with one stone. Nahler scrapes ton after ton of sand off of his land and dumps it onto the future levee site. But the process is slow, akin to shoveling snow off the driveway with a spoon, he said. In two weeks, Nahler has cleared about 10 acres. More than 400 acres await.

"I might not be able to put a crop here this year, but it's this or nothing," Nahler said.

The current forecast calls for a dry summer. "This time last year [during the flood] they were predicting a hot, dry summer, too," Williamson said. "I don't believe in forecasts anymore. I use the 'now cast,' which is looking out the window and seeing it's sunny and 70 degrees out. That's all you can bank on."

Excerpted from the *Columbia Missourian*, March 30, 1994

"If they'd spend as much money on levee repairs as they've spent sending people out here to look at it, maybe we could get somewhere," said Clifton Nahler, farmer.

Missouri River Mud

The River has many gifts, but mud has got to be one of its greatest treasures

By Marti Kardinal of Rocheport

❖

The Missouri River is probably the most underused natural resource in Mid-America. Even the towns tend to turn their backs on it, though when it comes to push and shove the Missouri River is surely something to reckon with. If you really want to know the river, you'd best get as close as you can. If you're in a boat, make it low enough where you can dip your hand into the water and see what the river has swallowed up, for nothing but brown can be seen more than a quarter inch down.

In warm summer months the Missouri River runs like murky soup, half-land, half-water — and mud. As her water level lowers, she slows, leaving fine silky stuff stuck to the banks — slick and slippery black mud. Nothing is smoother or more cool and soothing to the touch, especially to a sun-baked skin. Applied liberally, it prevents sunburn. Smeared on in artistic abandon, it can make fantastic body designs. It is so pure in consistency it could be bottled up, have a fancy label put on and be sold for a good profit as a truly natural beauty mask.

In the late summer as the mud dries it forms intricate geometric patterns across the flats. The cracks run deep to the cooler wetter zone where life can be found. Newly deposited mud is no good for walking. More trouble than it's worth. Ancient mud is what is really valuable. When you dig down a little further you get to some of the firmer stuff. That's clay. If you're caught out on the river and have to sleep over on an island, you can make all the pots and bowls you want, just like the Native Americans did. Fire them up hard in your campfire. It works.

Look out onto the flood plains, to where the eye almost greets the horizon, to appreciate the great bounty that flows off the land and to our tables. This is based, wouldn't you know, on the thick, black soil called gumbo, brought here by the river, made black and rich by Missouri's Ultimate Delight — MUD!

For More Information:

Interactive Katy Trail Internet Site: www.katytrail.showmestate.com
Missouri Department of Conservation publications, Missouri Department of
  Conservation, P.O. Box 180, Jefferson City, MO 65102.
Off the Beaten Path, Touring Cyclist, 11816 St. Charles Rock Road, Bridgeton,
  MO 63044.
The Complete Katy Trail Guidebook, Pebble Publishing, P.O. Box 431,
  Columbia, MO 65205.
The River Valley Companion — A Nature Guide, Pebble Publishing,
  P.O. Box 431, Columbia, MO 65205.
Visit the **Greater St. Charles Visitors Bureau** online at: www.st-charles.mo.us
Steamboat Arabia Museum • 400 Grand Ave. • KC, MO 64106 • www.1856.com
Visit the **Touring Cyclist bike shop** online at http://www.tcyclist.com
  or call (573) 739-5180. Leave e-mail at info@tcyclist.com
Rails-to-Trails Conservancy • 1400 Sixteenth Street, NW Suite 300
  Washington, DC 20036 • (202) 797-5400
Department of Natural Resources • Division of State Parks
  P.O. Box 176 • Jefferson City, MO 65102
  (314) 751-2479 or 1 (800) 334-6946 or 1 (800) 379-2419 (with TDD)
  www.state.mo.us/dnr/dsp/homedesp.htm
Division of Tourism • P.O. Box 1055
  Jefferson City, MO 65102 • (314) 751-4133
The Access Fund (to support rock-climbing along the trail)
  P.O. Box 17010 • Boulder, CO 80308-9804
Missouri Trails and Streams • Bill Oliver • (314) 458-1995
Katy Trail State Park Update Newsletter (Free)
  Missouri Department of Natural Resources
  Division of State Parks • P.O. Box 176
  Jefferson City, MO 65102 • Call toll free: 1 (800) 334-6946
Visit the **Lewis and Clark keelboat** online at discovery.showmestate.com

Bibliographical Resources

James M. Denny. "History and Cultural Resources Along the Katy Railroad Corridor: Sedalia to Clinton Section." Unpublished report prepared for Missouri Department of Natural Resources, Division of Parks, Recreation and Historic Preservation, November, 1991.

James M. Denny. "Manitou Bluffs Section of the Missouri River." Manitou Publications, 1996. Rt. 1, Box 3810, Jamestown, MO 65046.

James M. Denny, Gerald Lee Gilleard, and Joetta K. Davis. "Cultural Resources along the Missouri, Kansas and Texas (Katy Trail) Railroad Route, Sedalia to Machens, Missouri." Unpublished report prepared for Missouri Department of Natural Resources, Division of Parks, Recreation and Historic Preservation, September, 1986.

Brett Dufur. "Sojourn of Sorrow." *The River Valley Review,* Pebble Publishing, Columbia, MO, 1995.

Bob Dyer's *Big Canoe Songbook: Ballads from the Heartland* provided some of the most useful and succinctly written information on the history of this region, including tips on when to write "Boone's Lick" versus "Boonslick." Also, his music adds a greatly needed lyrical dimension to the normally very dry two-dimensional interpretation of history.

Lee N. Godley. *Callaway Keys to the Kingdom.* Aphelion Publications, Fulton, MO, 1994.

George Kennedy, the editor of the *Columbia Missourian,* graciously granted reprint permission for the *Columbia Missourian* articles reprinted in this book.

V.V. Masterson. *The KATY Railroad and the Last Frontier.* Norman: University of Oklahoma Press, 1952.

Floyd Shoemaker. *Missouri and Missourians.* Vol. 1. Lewis Publishing Company. Chicago. 1943.

"Town Restores Discarded Caboose to Its Patriotic Splendor," and "Additional Details on Windsor, Missouri's Katy Caboose (Spirit of 76.)" *The Katy Flyer* 13 (March 1991), p. 14.

Photo Credits and Illustrations

R. C. Adams: p. 78, 86. Terry Barner: front cover, pp. 65, 98. Nhat Meyer. p. 50. Julie Pomerantz: pp. 137, all on 139. Keith Simonsen: pp. 87, 95. Brian Storm: p. 154. Steve Wright: three color photos on back cover. All other photos by the author. Friends of Historic Rocheport granted reprint permission for photos in the **Trails of Dust** section.

Illustrator Kerri Mulvania has also worked at excavation sites in Belize, Central America, on grants and is now working on her PhD in Philosophy in Boulder, Colorado. Thanks to Martin Bellmann and Tawnee Brown, whose work is on pages 57 and 103 respectively.

About the Author

Brett Dufur is the author of *The Complete Katy Trail Guidebook, Best of Missouri Hands* and the *River Valley Companion.* He is also co-author of *Exploring Missouri Wine Country* and *Forgotten Missourians Who Made History.* In addition to books, he is the founder, editor and publisher of Pebble Publishing, based in Rocheport, Missouri.

ZAP! Missouri's Katy Trail now accessible from cyberspace

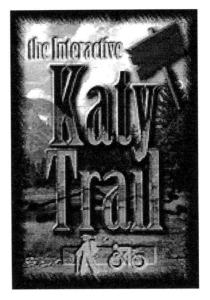

P arts of the *Katy Trail Guidebook* are now available in an online edition, called the **Interactive Katy Trail**, opening up the trail to 10 million "cyberhikers" worldwide, who surf the Internet for fun and information.

The site was developed by Global Image, Inc., an award-winning producer of sites on the Internet's World-Wide Web, and Pebble Publishing.

The online guide, the first and most complete online rails-to-trails to hit the Internet, includes updates on trail conditions, area day trips and lots of gorgeous color photographs. There are also forums where people can meet, ask questions, and talk about things like hiking, biking and where to find a place to stay.

Thousands of visitors have surfed by the site since its launch in December 1995. The site's designer, Alan Westenbroek, said, "We've received e-mail from people around the world who are planning trips to Missouri to check out the trail. Groups from other states have visited, who want to use the trail as a model for their own Rails-to-Trails projects."

Since the **Interactive Katy Trail** was launched, its innovative, content-packed design has garnered numerous awards, including mentions in *USA Today,* Point Communications' **Top 5 Percent of the Web award, Editor's Choice in Reader's Digest,** an award from **Gateway Trailnet** in St. Louis, and was ranked as one of **PC Computing's Top 1,001 Internet Sites.** Dufur says he attributes the number of awards to the site's graphics, easy navigation and striking photography.

For people thinking about a vacation or adventure in Missouri this spring, the **Interactive Katy Trail** is a perfect starting point. The **Interactive Katy Trail** is accessible on the Internet's World-Wide Web at:

katytrail.showmestate.com

Coupons not valid if removed. Each business will mark the coupon for validation at time of use.

$1 OFF 2-HOUR BIKE RENTAL

(Any style)

——————— Trailside Cafe ———————
Bike Rental, Sales and Service

Full service bike sales and rental including
Raleigh, Nishiki and GT. Bikes of various sizes and speeds.
Mountain Bikes. Single Speeds. Bike Accessories.
Tandems. Child Seats. Pull carts. Side by Side 3-Wheelers.
Burley carts and more.

Something for all ages!

(573) 698-2702 or (573) 445-6361
At Rocheport Trailhead • 1st and Pike
Reservations accepted but not necessary. Visa, MC and Discover.

10% off
Historic Bed & Breakfast Mansion
Monday — Thursday

——— Rivercene B&B ———

Between Boonville and New Franklin

The Rivercene Bed and Breakfast, owned by Jody and Ron Lenz, was built in 1864, built from materials from all over the world — imported Italian marble for the nine fireplaces, black walnut for the front doors and hand-carved mahogany for the staircase. Rivercene is ideal for resting and relaxing after your ride on the Katy Trail.

How to Get There: Rivercene is located north of Boonville, and a half mile from the Katy Trail on the north side of the Missouri River. From I-70, take Exit 103, and go north through Boonville, cross the river and turn right on the first road - County Road 463. Rivercene is located a quarter of a mile east.

Call (816) 848-2497 and 1 (800) 531-0862
for reservations, brochures or other information.

Coupons not valid if removed. Each business will mark the coupon for validation at time of use.

The Show Me Missouri Series

99 Fun Things to Do
in Columbia & Boone County
ISBN: 0-9646625-2-3

Guide to 99 hidden highlights, unique dining, galleries, museums, towns, people and history in Columbia, Rocheport, Centralia and Boone County. Most trips are free or under $10. Includes maps, photos, accessibility of sites. Fully indexed. 168 pages. By Pamela Watson. $12.95

A to Z Missouri
ISBN: 0-9646625-4-X

Abo to Zwanzig! A dictionary-style book of Missouri place name origins. Includes history for each town and community, pronunciations, population, county, post office dates and more. 220 pages. By Margot Ford McMillen. $14.95

Daytrip Missouri
ISBN: 0-9651340-0-8

Information on tourist attractions throughout the state. Topics include history, up-to-date attraction information, a listing of annual events and helpful travel tips for more than 40 locations around the state, and travel notes by Missouri tourism directors. In addition, 60 black and white photos and 20 maps make this the tour guide standard for Missouri. 224 pages. By Lee N. Godley and Patricia Murphy O'Rourke. $14.95

Exploring Missouri Wine Country
ISBN: 0-9646625-6-6

This guidebook to Missouri wine country offers an intimate look at Missouri's winemakers and wineries, including how to get there, their histories and the story of how Missouri came to have its own Rhineland. Includes wine tips, recipes, home-brew recipes, dictionary of wine terms and more. Also lists nearby Bed and Breakfasts and lodging. 168 pages. By Brett Dufur and Mark Flakne. $14.95

Forgotten Missourians Who Made History
ISBN: 0-9646625-8-2

A book of short stories and humorous comic-style illustrations of more than 35 Missourians who made a contribution to the state or nation yet are largely forgotten by subsequent generations. By Jim Borwick and Brett Dufur. $14.95

The Show Me Missouri Series

The Complete Katy Trail Guidebook   ISBN: 0-9646625-0-7

The most complete guide to services, towns, people, places and history along Missouri's 200-mile Katy Trail. This updated edition covers the cross-state hiking and biking trail from Clinton to St. Charles — now America's longest rails-to-trails project. Includes trailhead maps, 80 photos, Flood of '93, how to make blueberry wine, uses for Missouri mud and more. 168 pages. By Brett Dufur. $14.95

River Rat's Guide to Missouri River Folklore and History

This book is *THE CLASSIC* on Missouri River history and folklore. Documented bend by bend by one of the river's greatest admirers — river rat and historian Cecil Griffith. Throughout his 36 years at the Corps of Engineers, he compiled tales and history about the River, river town folklore, snags, great riverboat calamities and more. Originally published in 1974. Now reissued with all new maps, illustrations, index and more. Compiled by Cecil Griffith. 144 pages. $14.95

The River Revisited — In the Wake of Lewis and Clark

Includes journal entries from the original voyage, as well as modern day commentary on the river and how it has been affected in the 200 years since Lewis and Clark — ecologically, socially and culturally. Includes pull-out map of the Missouri River, 50 photos and journals from last summer's modern-day crew of reenactors. 224 pages. By Brett Dufur. $16.95 ISBN: 0-9646625-9-0

River Valley Companion — A Nature Guide ISBN: 0-9646625-1-5

Companion to the *Katy Trail Guidebook*. A nice balance between nature, science and fun. This easy-to-use, illustrated four-season guide identifies commonly seen trees, flowers, birds, animals, insects, rocks, fossils, clouds, reptiles, footprints and more. Features the Missouri River Valley's most outstanding sites and nature daytrips. 176 pages. Compiled by Brian Beatte and Brett Dufur. $14.95

Wit & Wisdom of Missouri's Country Editors

A compilation of over 600 pithy sayings from pioneer Missouri newspapers. Many of these quotes and quips date to the 19th century yet remain timely for today's readers. Richly illustrated and fully indexed to help you find that perfect quote. 168 pages. By William Taft. $14.95 ISBN: 0-9646625-3-1

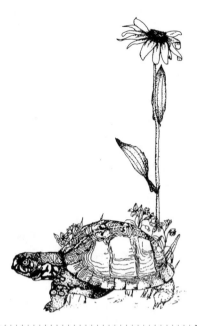

how Me Missouri books are available at many local bookstores. They can also be ordered directly from the publisher, using this form, or ordered by phone, fax or over the Internet.

Pebble Publishing also distributes 100 other books of regional interest, Rails-To-Trails, Missouri history, heritage, nature, recreation and more. These are available through our online bookstore and mail-order catalog.

Visit our online bookstore, *Trailside Books,* on the Internet at www.trailsidebooks.com. If you would like to receive our catalog, please fill out and mail the form on this page.

Pebble Publishing

P.O. Box 431 ❖ Columbia, MO 65205-0431
(800) 576-7322 ❖ Fax: (573) 698-3108

Quantity	*Book Title*	*x Unit Price =*	*Total*

Mo. residents add 6.975% sales tax = ------------
Shipping ($1.24 each book) x = ------------
Total = ------------

Name:_____

Email Address:_____

Address:_____ Apt._____

City, State, Zip_____

Phone: (_____) _____

Credit Card # _____

Expiration Date _____/_____/_____   Please send catalog _____

Visit ***Trailside Books*** online at http://www.trailsidebooks.com